Jesus is Better

My Notes on Hebrews

By

Dr. T. John Dell

Word of His Mouth Publishers
Mooresboro, NC

All Scripture quotations are taken from the **King James Version** of the Bible.

ISBN: 978-1-941039-43-4
Printed in the United States of America
©2016 Dr. T. John Dell

Word of His Mouth Publishers
Mooresboro, NC 28114
www.wordofhismouth.com

CONTENTS

MY NOTES ON HEBREWS

I have always loved the book of Hebrews. Of course, I love all the books of the Bible. I've not always studied the Bible like I should, nor like I want to. Truly my spirit is willing, but sometimes my flesh is weak.

I started teaching through the book of Hebrews during our Wednesday night Bible study at Murrayville Baptist Church. I began the study October 15, 2014 and finished April 13, 2016. I thank God for the opportunity to teach His Word and I also thank the Lord for the faithful people of our church. We have other ministries that operate on Wednesday nights (AWANA) and many of our people work with our young people within this program. The people who come on Wednesday night to Bible study are my heroes. They come faithfully and eager to learn God's Word. It has been my God given opportunity to teach some of the finest saints of God in the world. I know every pastor feels this way about his own people, and rightfully so. The saints who gather on Wednesday nights come in tired from their day, facing problems that only God can fix, but yet they come. They are my heroes.

I have never taught through a book of the Bible verse by verse at MBC until I taught through the book of Hebrews. The Lord led me to do so, and the study has enriched my life and helped me grow in grace and in the knowledge of my Savior.

The following are simply my notes as I studied and prepared. It is not a commentary. Most of these teachings may be found recorded on our church website under the "Media" tab @ www.murrayvillebaptist.org. There are verses referenced that you will have to look up and some verses printed within the notes. My prayer is that these "notes" will aid you in your Bible study time. If you do use these notes and notice any errors or have any questions, please email me and let me know @ tjohndell@murrayvillebaptist.org.

2 Thessalonians 3:1 Finally, brethren, pray for us, that the word of the Lord may have *free* course, and be glorified, even as *it is* with you:

God Bless,

Dr. T John Dell, Pastor
Murrayville Baptist Church
5407 Hubert Stephens Road
Murrayville, GA 30564

The Book of Hebrews

INTRODUCTION

The book of Hebrews is the only book that DETAILS the present ministry of Jesus. The four gospels DECLARE what Jesus did on earth; Hebrews DESCRIBES what Jesus is doing now in Heaven.

Titles of Jesus in Hebrews:
Author – 12:2
The Apostle – 3:1
Captain – 2:10; 12:2
Christ – 3:6
Finisher – 12:2
Firstborn – 1:6
Forerunner – 6:20
God – 1:8
Heir – 1:2
High Priest – 2:17
Lord – 2:3
Mediator – 8:6
Shepherd – 13:20
Son – 1:2
Surety – 7:22

13 chapters; 303 verses; 6913 words

Key Words

"Jesus" – 14 times – 2:9; 3:1; 4:8; 4:14; 6:20; 7:22; 10:10; 10:19; 12:2; 12:24; 13:8; 13:12; 13:20

"Better" – 13 times – Resurrection (11:35); Country (11:16); Things (11:40); Hope (7:19); Sacrifices (9:23); Promises (8:6); Covenant (8:6); Substance (10:34); Jesus better than the angels (1:4)

5   Warning Passages

1) 2:1-4 – Disregarding the Salvation of God
Those who disregard the salvation of God are spiritual losers.
2) 3:1-4:11 – Disbelieving the Sufficiency of God
There is a rest for the believer. Many never find: joy, peace, rest, victory that Jesus has obtained for us.
3) 6:1-20 – Discrediting the Steadfastness of God
It pays to serve Jesus; those who quit will never inherit the promises.
4) 10:19-39 – Despising the Son of God
We are covenant people and drawing back from that covenant will bring the chastening of God.
5) 12:1-29 – Disobeying the Service of God
When God tells you to do something, you best do it. Esau despised his birthright; his privilege. He wanted the world's benefits and had no sense of spiritual values. He traded away spiritual and eternal benefits for temporary sensual indulgences (12:15-17). Hebrews deals with the reality of the consequences of not serving God. After all is done on earth, what will you have in the kingdom?

Key Verse

Hebrews 6:1 – going on unto perfection in the Christian life.
Perfection - "maturity; completeness; finisher"
Php 1:6 Being confident of this very thing, that he which hath begun a good work in you will perform *it* until the day of Jesus Christ:

Heb 12:2 Looking unto Jesus the author and finisher of *our* faith; who for the joy that was set before him endured the cross, despising the shame, and is set down at the right hand of the throne of God.

Theme of the Book

Jesus makes everything better!

CHAPTER 1

Verse 1

Sundry – "more than 1 or 2; bits and pieces" (ill) Settle's Sundry Store

Isa 28:10 For precept *must be* upon precept, precept upon precept; line upon line, line upon line; here a little, *and* there a little:

Various times and different manners – Angels; men; jackass; dreams; visions; judges; prophets; kings; shepherds; herdmen; Amos, a gatherer of sycamore fruits

Verse 2

Spoken – 2:2-3; 12:25-26; 2 Pet 1:16:21; Heb 6:18 The Word – Ps 103:20

Num 23:19 God *is* not a man, that he should lie; neither the son of man, that he should repent: hath he said, and shall he not do *it*? or hath he spoken, and shall he not make it good?

Heir – "one who is entitled to possess" Matt 21:33-46; Rom 8:17; Gal 4:6-7; Titus 3:7; Heb 1:14

Made the Worlds – John 1:3; Col 1:13-17; Rev 3:14

Verse 3

Brightness of His glory – Ex 33:18-23; John 1:14; John 17:24; 2 Cor 4:6

(ill) Moses – Ex 33:11; Deut 5:4 – Face to face - "to encounter; come in contact with"

Express image – "plain; clear; exact representative" John 14:9 this is why making images is forbidden

Ex 20:4 Thou shalt not make unto thee any graven image, or any likeness *of any thing* that *is* in heaven above, or that *is* in the earth beneath, or that *is* in the water under the earth: Rom 1:23 And changed the glory of the uncorruptible God into an image made like to corruptible man, and to birds, and fourfooted beasts, and creeping things. Col 1:15 Who is the image of the invisible God, the firstborn of every creature:

Man was made in the "image" of God and lost this image in the garden – Gen 1:27; Gen 5:3; Rom 8:29; 1 Cor 15:49; 2 Cor 3:18; Ps 17:15

Upholding all things – "to sustain; to keep from falling; to maintain" Heb 11:3; 2 Pet 3:3-7

Purged our sins – "to carry off impurities; to purify; to cleanse; evacuated" God just forgiving your sins is not enough; your sins must be purged; Ex 34:5-7. The purging of your sins will clear your guilt; your conscience – Heb 9:14; Ps 65:3-4; Ps 79:9-10; John 15:1-3; 2 Pet 1:9

The purging of our sins took place when Christ applied His blood on the mercy seat

Heb 9:11-12; John 20:16-17, 19-20

Luke 24:36-39 In one sentence He goes from creation to Calvary

Sat down – Heb 10:12…only one time said to stand – Acts 7:55-56

(ill) Dad asked little girl what she learned in Sunday school. "God is left handed…Jesus is sitting on his right hand"

Verse 4
More excellent name – Phil 2:8-11

Verse 8
Ps 45:6-7

Thy throne – God will have no one touching His throne unless permission is granted. God is jealous over His throne. Not just a symbol of power and position, but it is the power and position of the universe. The battle of the ages has been over this throne. Isa 14

Lucifer wanted his throne to be exalted above the throne of God. The throne of God is established forever. A billion, billion years from now the Lord will be sitting upon His throne with no decay, deathless in His energy, and presiding over the destinies of the ages to come.

There are some that will be able to approach this throne, Rev 3:21-22

Verse 9
Oil of gladness – "much rejoicing; leaping for joy" Lk 15:7, 10; Isa 53:11; Heb 12:2

Verse 10
Works of thine hands – Isa 40:12: Job 38:3-6

Verse 11
Ps 102:26; Ps 104:1-2; Isa 40:22

Verse 13
God has never invited an angel to come sit in His throne; but there are some that will have the INVITATION from Jesus to come and sit in the throne of the universe; Rev 3:21-22

Verse 14
Isa 36:21-22; 37:15-20, 36; 2 Kings 6:15-17; Matt 18:10; Heb 13:2

Lessons Learned
The Superiority of Jesus

Jesus: 1) Outspeaks the Prophets 2) Outranks the Angels 3) Outlasts the Universe

CHAPTER 2

Since Jesus is superior to all humans, spirits, and material things, we must appropriate the salvation that God has given us to our lives. Heb 6:9 This is the 1st of 5 warnings in Hebrews.

Verse 1

Earnest – "more abundant; more frequent"

Heed – "be cautious about; pay attention to; have regard for; apply oneself to; to hold the mind"

Slip – "carelessly pass or miss; to flow by"

The word "Heed" is interesting to study

"Take Heed" (in NT)

Acts 20:28 Take heed therefore unto yourselves, and to all the flock, over the which the Holy Ghost hath made you overseers, to feed the church of God, which he hath purchased with his own blood. 1 Cor 3:10 According to the grace of God which is given unto me, as a wise masterbuilder, I have laid the foundation, and another buildeth thereon. But let every man take heed how he buildeth thereupon. 1 Cor 8:9 But take heed lest by any means this liberty of yours become a stumblingblock to them that are weak. 1 Cor 10:12 Wherefore let him that thinketh he standeth take heed lest he fall. Gal 5:15 But if ye bite and devour one another, take heed that ye be not consumed one of another. 1 Tim 4:16 Take heed unto thyself, and unto the doctrine; continue in them: for in doing this thou shalt both save thyself, and them that hear thee. Heb 3:12 Take heed, brethren, lest there be in any of you an evil heart of unbelief, in departing from the living God.

But our text – "the more earnest heed" to the things which we have HEARD

Mark 4:23-25; Luke 8:18

2 Peter 1:15-21

Matt 13:15-17

1 John 2:6-7 He that saith he abideth in him ought himself also so to walk, even as he walked. Brethren, I write no new commandment unto you, but an old commandment which ye had from the beginning. The old commandment is the word which ye have heard from the beginning. 1 John 2:24 Let that therefore abide in you, which ye have heard from the beginning. If that which ye have heard from the beginning shall remain in you, ye also shall continue in the Son, and in the Father.

Verse 2

By angels – Gal 3:19; Acts 7:38, 53
(ill) Genesis 19:1, 11, 13, 16-17, 26-28
Just recompense – Ex 21:23-25; "substitute wages" God will pay you with a substitute. Not what He intended for your life
Rom 1:27
"You break my law, it will break you; you violate my law, it will violate you."

Verse 3

Escape – "to pass away from; to shun; to avoid harm"
Neglect – "to be careless of; not regard; to slight; to not notice; to make little of; to disregard; to show no interest in"
Neglect not Reject – "sinners reject salvation; saints neglect salvation"
Heb 10:28-30
Great – "of the greatest magnitude; so mighty"
It is a great salvation because: 1) Plan, man could never invent or imagine such a plan to deal with man's sin issue and provide a way that man could be forgiven by God. 2) Price 3) Provision (whosoever) 4) Power to change
Salvation – "deliverance; rescue; health"

Verse 5

The world to come – this phrase only appears 5 times in the Word of God, only in NT

Matt 12:32; Mark 10:30; Luke 18:30; Heb 6:5

2 Pet 3:6-7, 13 God has a 3 phase building program

The world to come will not be under the authority of the angels but under subjection of the reigning redeemed of this world.

1 Cor 6:2-3 Do ye not know that the saints shall judge the world? and if the world shall be judged by you, are ye unworthy to judge the smallest matters? Know ye not that we shall judge angels? how much more things that pertain to this life? Luke 12:32 Fear not, little flock; for it is your Father's good pleasure to give you the kingdom. Rev 20:4 And I saw thrones, and they sat upon them, and judgment was given unto them: and *I saw* the souls of them that were beheaded for the witness of Jesus, and for the word of God, and which had not worshipped the beast, neither his image, neither had received *his* mark upon their foreheads, or in their hands; and they lived and reigned with Christ a thousand years.

Verse 6

Psalms 8

Verse 7

Glory - "dignity; nobleness; elevation of grandeur" and Honor - "valuable; to esteem very precious"

Gen 1:26-31 One word stands out in this narrative –

Dominion - "to reign; to rule; to prevail against" This is what the devil could not stand. A created being of "lesser rank" freely given the dominion that Satan wanted.

Satan is so proud that he wants the title of "god of this world" and he is so proud that he wanted his throne to be above God's throne!!!! He wants glory and honor!

In the beginning man had the covering of "glory" and the power to dominate the universe. Ruling God's creation was man's God given privilege and power!

Verse 8

Everything was placed under the feet of man. Nothing was excluded.

"BUT NOW – we see – NOT YET" Why? Genesis 3 – Paradise Lost. Sin has robbed man of this dominion. Human beings DO NOT have control of this world YET!

Ever try to control a bird's flight in the air? Ever try to go under water indefinitely without equipment providing oxygen? There are sunken ships. There are wrecked cars. There are downed airplanes. We simply are not in control – YET!

Why? Man has fallen from that pedestal where God placed him. Now he is totally a lost sinner in need of a Savior. Man went from being clothed in the light of God's glory to clothing himself with leaves. MAN'S GLORY HAS BEEN LOST!

Verse 9

The CENTRAL verse for not only this chapter but the whole of Hebrews and of the entire Bible. Now the writer is fixing our hearts and eyes upon the One who came into this world and gives us 1) The Recourse of His Coming 2) The Regality of His Coming 3) The Reason of His Coming

John Phillips – "Jesus Christ was on the throne of the universe, yet He entered the narrow confines of the womb of a virgin. Jesus Christ, before whom the angels of God fell in worship, condescended below angelic nature and took upon Himself human nature."

Paul writes it like this: Php 2:5-8 Let this mind be in you, which was also in Christ Jesus: Who, being in the form of God, thought it not robbery to be equal with God: But made himself of no reputation, and took upon him the form of a servant, and was made in the likeness of men: And being found in fashion as a man, he humbled himself, and became obedient unto death, even the death of the cross.

* Jesus revealed the "glory of God" in His incarnation – John 1:14 We beheld his glory, the glory as of the only begotten of the Father, full of grace and truth.
* When Jesus performed miracles He was revealing the "glory of God."
(ill) Marriage of Cana, John 2:11 This beginning of miracles did Jesus in Cana of Galilee, and manifested forth his glory.
* Simon Peter could not get a bite after an all- nighter on the Sea of Galilee. Jesus said, "Cast your net on the right side for a draught." Word got out that the Creator of sea and fish needed some fish and every fish in that sea came swiftly to submit to His dominion.
* Because of sin came death and disease. Jesus stepped in front of every disease and in different manners healed every sickness and every disease. Fevers left without treating just the symptoms but healing the cause of the fever. Withered hands were completely made whole. Leprosy was instantly and completely cured. Death was counted as nothing when the Master and Lord of Creation stepped into its arena. The Son of God manifested God's glory and honor that gave Him dominion over everything. God wanted man to have dominion. But sin came, and man lost that dominion because he lost the glory and honor freely given him by God.

But the crowning revelation of the "glory of God" was found in the crucifixion of Jesus.
"A Baby Changes Everything" – those little feet will one day climb the hill to Calvary; those little hands will one day have horrific nails driven through them to secure Him to a cross; that perfect side will be pierced through with a spear and the piercer will declare, "Truly this was the Son of God." That little body

will one day mature into a 33-year-old man and die a horrible death. But this death will be like no other.

He TASTED death for every man.

Taste – "to try the relish of anything; to experience the fruits of" Why? The wages of sin is death. The only payment God will accept for our sin is the payment of death. When Jesus was dying on the cross, He was paying the penalty that our sins deserved. Christ tasted what we should taste. He experienced every drunken stupor, every drug induced intoxication, every rape, every murder, every bludgeoning, every torture, every lie, every fornication, every pain associated with every sin – Jesus in a six-hour period tasted it all! The separation caused by sin – "My God, my God Why hast thou forsaken me?"

Verse 10

The Supreme One did all of this so that He could restore man to His original intent – Glory!

Captain of their Salvation – "the one who founds a city or blazes the trail to a new found land."

Perfect - "qualified or complete"

The word "Glory" used three times in passage, 7, 9-10. We had it and lost it. Jesus has it and has made the way for us to get it back!

When we look at Jesus we are looking at what God gives us back at salvation.

John 17:22

Verse 11

One – John 17:19-23; John 10:28-30 And I give unto them eternal life; and they shall never perish, neither shall any *man* pluck them out of my hand. My Father, which gave *them* me, is greater than all; and no *man* is able to pluck *them* out of my Father's hand. I and *my* Father are one.

Sanctified – "to be made blameless; to be set apart from the rest"

When we receive Jesus Christ, we are sanctified by God. Positional sanctification

John 17:17-19; Eph 5:25-26; 2 Thes 2:13; 1 Cor 6:9-11

Rom 15:16 That I should be the minister of Jesus Christ to the Gentiles, ministering the gospel of God, that the offering up of the Gentiles might be acceptable, being sanctified by the Holy Ghost. 1 Thes 5:23 And the very God of peace sanctify you wholly; and *I pray God* your whole spirit and soul and body be preserved blameless unto the coming of our Lord Jesus Christ.

He is not ashamed – He knows who we are and what He has done in our lives. Even though we do things that shame His name, He is not ashamed of us.

Heb 11:16 But now they desire a better *country*, that is, an heavenly: wherefore God is not ashamed to be called their God: for he hath prepared for them a city. Rom 10:11 For the scripture saith, Whosoever believeth on him shall not be ashamed. Rom 1:16 For I am not ashamed of the gospel of Christ: for it is the power of God unto salvation to every one that believeth; to the Jew first, and also to the Greek. 2 Tim 1:12 For the which cause I also suffer these things: nevertheless I am not ashamed: for I know whom I have believed, and am persuaded that he is able to keep that which I have committed unto him against that day. 2 Tim 2:15 Study to shew thyself approved unto God, a workman that needeth not to be ashamed, rightly dividing the word of truth. 1 John 2:28 And now, little children, abide in him; that, when he shall appear, we may have confidence, and not be ashamed before him at his coming. Mark 8:38 Whosoever therefore shall be ashamed of me and of my words in this adulterous and sinful generation; of him also shall the Son of man be ashamed, when he cometh in the glory of his Father with the holy angels.

Why are we ashamed? 1) Pride 2) Disobedience 3) Lack of study on our part

Ashamed - "affected by shame" (1828)

Verses 12-13

Jesus is not ashamed of us in heaven's congregation, nor while we are upon earth. Why then should we be ashamed of Him?

Verse 14-18

He took part – which part? Romans 8:3; the flesh but not the blood

When you and I are born, we are comprised of flesh and blood. But when Jesus was born, He took part of the flesh for several reasons.

1) Death might be destroyed (14)

In the OT, because of the inadequacy of the OT sacrifices, saints did not go to heaven but to a place called Death, Abraham's bosom, Paradise. The devil had the power (the strength, the dominion) over death. Jesus Christ came and by means of death, He conquered death by His resurrection, and the devil had to relinquish the power.

Rev 1:18 *I am* he that liveth, and was dead; and, behold, I am alive for evermore, Amen; and have the keys of hell and of death. 2 Tim 1:10 But is now made manifest by the appearing of our Saviour Jesus Christ, who hath abolished death, and hath brought life and immortality to light through the gospel:

(ill) When David conquered Goliath, he took Goliath's own weapon and cut his head off. Jesus used the devil's own weapon and defeated him with it and His weapon of the resurrection is greater than death!

2) Deliverance from bondage (15)

Death is an enemy that entered this world through sin. It brings separation, sorrow, suffering, (ill) Preacher, "I'm not scared of death, but I am scared of dying."

1 Cor 15:26 The last enemy *that* shall be destroyed *is* death.

Rev 21:4 And God shall wipe away all tears from their eyes; and there shall be no more death, neither sorrow, nor crying, neither shall there be any more pain: for the former things are passed away.

3) The Divide between God and man might be reconciled (17)

Middle wall of separation

Job 9:32-33 For *he is* not a man, as I *am, that* I should answer him, *and* we should come together in judgment. Neither is there any daysman betwixt us, *that* might lay his hand upon us both.

The One who could rightfully bring man and God together had to be both. He had to fully be God and fully be man and Jesus Christ took on the likeness of sinful flesh that He might lay one hand on a Holy God and the other hand on a sinful man and bring the two together in reconciled relationship!

4) To Discover what it means to be tempted

He was tempted personally and powerfully by the devil. He was tempted by Simon Peter to bypass the cross (that be far from thee). He was tempted by his family, friends, familiars. He was despised and rejected, a man of sorrows and grief. He came unto His own and His own received Him not.

Tempted - "to be scrutinized; to be enticed; to be examined; to be proven"

"If you're the Christ, come down from the cross and save yourself."

Heb 4:15 For we have not an high priest which cannot be touched with the feeling of our infirmities; but was in all points tempted like as *we are, yet* without sin.

So Jesus is able to SUCCOUR - "to relieve or aid from difficulty, want or distress"

1 Cor 10:13 There hath no temptation taken you but such as is common to man: but God *is* faithful, who will not suffer you to be tempted above that ye are able; but will with the temptation also make a way to escape, that ye may be able to bear *it*.

The problem with us, there are certain temptations we enjoy, they appeal to us. We enjoy entertaining the thoughts, the ideas, the imaginations or the temptation and do not rather see the

23

underlying, beguiling, subtil enemy trying to lead us into something that will break us and break the heart of our Savior. What are we to do with our temptations?

(Heb 4:14-16)

1) Hold fast our profession – I'm a child of God

2) Realize that there is Someone to help; we are not alone

3) Come boldly and ask for help to overcome

Jas 1:12 Blessed *is* the man that endureth temptation: for when he is tried, he shall receive the crown of life, which the Lord hath promised to them that love him.

Lessons Learned

1) The Saint's DESTINY is the world to come

2) The Saint's DISTINCTION is seen in the way God visits us

3) The Saint's DIGNITY is the fact that Jesus is not ashamed of us

4) The Saint's DELIVERANCE from temptation is Jesus

CHAPTER 3

Verse 1

Christians have a 1) Holy Character 2) Heavenly Calling – in contrast to the Jews whose calling was earthly. In the OT, for the Jew to be ensured and enjoy the earthly blessings they had to be in the land. Whenever the Jew wandered outside of the land, they were punished and cut off from the blessings associated with the land. In the NT, for the Christian to be ensured and able to enjoy the heavenly blessings we have to remain in the Lord. Outside of Christ there is no blessing, only punishment and correction.

Consider - "discover; observe fully"

The whole theme of Hebrews points us to Jesus Christ. Chapter 1 describes and sets forth the superiority of Jesus Christ. Chapter 2, "But we see Jesus". Later in chapter 12, "Looking unto Jesus the author and finisher of our faith. Now, in Chapter 3, "Let us consider."

Apostle – one that represents God to man

High Priest – one that represents man to God

Profession – "the business which one professes to understand and follow"

Jerry Vines, *The Believer's Guide to Hebrews:*

> "First of all, we are 'holy brethren.' The word holy means 'set apart.' Brethren means 'brothers and sisters in the same family.' We are holy brothers and sisters in the family of God. We belong to God now and partake of the divine nature. We have been set apart. Our lives are not our own.
>
> "We are also 'partakers of the heavenly calling.' To partake means 'to have something in

common,' or in other words 'to be partners.' This phrase from Hebrews 3:1 explains why a doctor and a laborer, the rich and the poor, gather in the same meeting. They are now partners in a heavenly calling. They have something in common that brings them together.

"For many years church-growth experts have been making surveys and writing books. They study what makes churches grow. They give advice to churches concerning growth. These experts say that a church that will grow is one that is made up of the same kind of folks. In other words, if a church in a rich area is to grow, it has to minister to the rich. Or if a church in a poor area is to grow, it has to minister to the poor. These experts say you can't grow a church with all kinds of individuals.

"I say these experts are absolutely wrong. I say that a true genuine church that operates on the basis of the teachings of the Word of God is a church that brings people together around a common allegiance to the Lord Jesus Christ. We don't have fellowship on the basis of the material things we have or do not have. We are not drawn together on the basis of our social standings or intellectual endowments. Rather, we are all partakers of a heavenly calling, an upward calling."

Verse 2
Numbers 12:7
Moses was Israel's Apostle; the one that represented God to the Jews

Aaron was Israel's High Priest; the one that represented the Jew to God

But now Jesus does both – He represents God to us and represents us to God

(The devil accuses God to us and accuses us to God!)

Verse 2-5

Moses was a servant and found faithful in: 1) **Trust**; as a leader of God's people 2) **Talent**s; used the gifts God had given him for the ongoing of the nation 3) **Tests**; burning bush, face-off with Pharaoh, Red Sea Crossing

Yet, in all of this Moses was only a TYPE, an EXAMPLE, a FORESHADOW of the One to come, Jesus Christ, who was counted worthy of more glory than Moses.

(You talk to a Jew about Moses, Abraham, David and they will swell with pride to be of that lineage and have that heritage. But the writer of Hebrews is reminding and reaffirming to the Hebrews that Jesus is greater than Moses, their Leader!)

Verse 6

As a Son - Moses was faithful as a "servant" but Jesus was faithful as a son.

House – How is the house built? Matt 16:18 Jesus builds it, BUT we have a part in it also

1 Cor 2:9-12; Matt 7:24-27; 1 Pet 2:1-5; Phil 2:12-14

IF – If we keep our confidence in the work of God in our lives, we will remain faithful IN the Lord and TO the Lord.

Jesus has committed Himself to every Christian, but not every Christian has committed themselves to Jesus.

Gal 5:24; Rom 8:5, 8; Phil 3:17-19

Abiding in Christ is a MUST for growth and fruit bearing – John 15

Abide - "to continue; to stay put; to dwell; to endure; to remain; to stay still"

Verse 8

Provocation - "to excite; to stimulate; to arouse; to irritate; to make angry; to offend; to enrage"

Hard Heart – against God making you grow and stay faithful. "I don't like change" mentality.

2 Cor 3:14-18

Erring Heart – not knowing the ways of the Lord

Evil Heart – unbelief; departing from the Living God

Rom 8:28-29 And we know that all things work together for good to them that love God, to them who are the called according to *his* purpose. For whom he did foreknow, he also did predestinate *to be* conformed to the image of his Son, that he might be the firstborn among many brethren.

Ps 78:1-17, 32-42
Ps 106:7-15, 21, 24, 29

The Lord wants us to REST in Him! It grieves the Lord when one of His children will not trust Him and rest in His saving work! Many Christians are saved, they have not lost their salvation; but they have lost their Joy, Peace, Fellowship, Faith, Hope all because they have lost their CONFIDENCE in their Lord!

Bumper Sticker – "Made for More"

Lessons Learned

1) Jesus is everything we need in our relationship with God
2) Just living a second rate Christian life is not enough
3) Judgment is awaiting the Christian who hardens his heart against God

CHAPTER 4

The child of God can fail as miserably as the children of Israel did in the wilderness.

The Wilderness experiences in our lives are necessary on our way into the promised land of rest in Jesus. What the wilderness was to Israel, the world is to the Christian. God has so much that is better for us than what this world has to offer.

Wilderness experiences with your: 1) Home 2) Finances 3) Desires 4) Relationship with God 5) Relationship with others 6) Worship 7) Faith

The Wilderness: 1) A Barren Experience 2) A Bewildering Experience 3) A Beckoning Experience

In the wilderness they did see the supernatural miracles of God performed on their behalf: Manna, water, glory of God; but all of that was to lead them on into maturity and restful reliance in the Lord.

(ill) 3 million Jews left Egypt on that fateful night of the Passover. Moses would have to have had 1500 tons of food each day. Do you know that to bring that much food each day, two freight trains, each at least a mile long, would be required! (Water) If they only had enough to drink and wash a few dishes, it would take 11,000,000 gallons each day and a freight train with tank cars, 1800 miles long, just to bring water! (Red Sea) So there had to be a space in the Red Sea, 3 miles wide so that they could walk 5000 abreast to get over in one night. Land size needed to accommodate everyone and their stuff – 750 square miles; 2/3 the size of the state of Rhode Island. Moses did not sit down and calculate all of this beforehand, God just took care of it.

But the nation of Israel did not express faith – they lacked faith which bred: murmuring, complaining, disbelief on their part.
1 Corinthians 10:1-13

Verse 1-2

There were two things missing in the Jews lives – fear and faith.

Fear – It's been said that fear is an unhealthy emotion, but: Prov 1:7 The fear of the LORD *is* the beginning of knowledge: *but* fools despise wisdom and instruction. 2 Tim 1:7 For God hath not given us the spirit of fear; but of power, and of love, and of a sound mind.

How do you reconcile those two? Simple – we choose to fear everything except the Lord or either we fear the Lord and nothing else.

Fear has a negative connotation;

Webster's 1828 – "a painful emotion or passion excited by an expectation of evil or the apprehension of impending danger" "to be afraid of"

Some worry about everything showing a lack of trust in the Lord.

Our Past, Our Present, Our Future

(ill) St. Patrick said – "It is distrust of God to be troubled over what is to come. It is impatience with God to be troubled with what is present, and it is anger at God to be troubled over what has passed."

1) Fearing God is a choice a person makes: Prov 1:29 For that they hated knowledge, and did not choose the fear of the LORD:

2) Who should fear God? Ps 33:8-9 Let all the earth fear the LORD: let all the inhabitants of the world stand in awe of him. For he spake, and it was *done*; he commanded, and it stood fast.

3) When a man fears God, he fears nothing else: Ps 27:1-3 *A Psalm* of David. The LORD *is* my light and my salvation; whom shall I fear? the LORD *is* the strength of my life; of whom shall I be afraid? When the wicked, *even* mine enemies and my foes, came upon me to eat up my flesh, they stumbled and fell. Though an host should encamp against me, my heart shall not fear: though war should rise against me, in this *will* I *be* confident.

4) The early church feared God: Acts 5:11 And great fear came upon all the church, and upon as many as heard these things. Acts 9:31 Then had the churches rest throughout all Judaea and Galilee and Samaria, and were edified; and walking in the fear of the Lord, and in the comfort of the Holy Ghost, were multiplied.

5) Fear of God will clean up your life: 2 Cor 7:1 Having therefore these promises, dearly beloved, let us cleanse ourselves from all filthiness of the flesh and spirit, perfecting holiness in the fear of God.

6) People will not submit to others because they don't fear God: Eph 5:21 Submitting yourselves one to another in the fear of God.

7) Christians will not live for God because they don't fear God: Php 2:12 Wherefore, my beloved, as ye have always obeyed, not as in my presence only, but now much more in my absence, work out your own salvation with fear and trembling.

(ill) Noah, Heb 11:7 By faith Noah, being warned of God of things not seen as yet, moved with fear, prepared an ark to the saving of his house; by the which he condemned the world, and became heir of the righteousness which is by faith.

Fearing things, circumstances, worry is a SIN!

That lack of fear wrought a lack of faith in them:

Faith Heb 11:1 Now faith is the substance of things hoped for, the evidence of things not seen.

Just as faith is essential to bring us to salvation; faith is needed to bring us into the fullness that is in Christ.

Can't mix preaching with: 1) Feelings – Matt 13:20-21 But he that received the seed into stony places, the same is he that heareth the word, and anon with joy receiveth it; Yet hath he not root in himself, but dureth for a while: for when tribulation or persecution ariseth because of the word, by and by he is offended. 2) Doubt - Matt 21:21 Jesus answered and said unto them, Verily I say unto you, If ye have faith, and doubt not, ye shall not only do this *which is done* to the fig tree, but also if ye shall say unto this mountain, Be thou removed, and be thou cast into the sea; it shall be done. 3) Tradition - Matt 15:6 And honour not his father or his mother, *he shall be free*. Thus have ye made the commandment of God of none effect by your tradition.

Promises – "a declaration, either in writing or verbal, made by one person to another, which binds the person who makes it either in honor, conscience or law, to do a certain act specified; a declaration which gives to the person to whom it is made, a right to expect or claim the performance of the act;"
(ill) Moses would "remind" God of His promises made. In essence, he was not reminding God of what He said but expressing faith (expectancy) in what God said.

2 Cor 1:20 For all the promises of God in him *are* yea, and in him Amen, unto the glory of God by us.
What is the land called that God promised to take them into? THE PROMISED LAND!

Numbers 13:17-33; Numbers 14:1-10
3 Reports 1) Giants 2) Grasshoppers 3) God

Short – "inferior; destitute; come behind; to be in want; suffer need; not of long duration"
Gal 6:9 And let us not be weary in well doing: for in due season we shall reap, if we faint not. Heb 6:11-12 And we desire that every one of you do shew the same diligence to the full assurance of hope unto the end: That ye be not slothful, but followers of them who through faith and patience inherit the promises.
Good is the enemy of Best. Many Christians have the idea that failing to be all that God wants us to be is really not that serious.

We develop the mindset, that they are going to heaven and it really doesn't matter how we live our lives down here.

(ill) "Well, that's just the way I am."

Profit - "to be useful; to benefit; to have the advantage; to be better; to prevail;" Isa 48:17 Thus saith the LORD, thy Redeemer, the Holy One of Israel; I *am* the LORD thy God which teacheth thee to profit, which leadeth thee by the way *that* thou shouldest go.

In this chapter this is the first of three sets of "Let us therefore"

Let us therefore fear (1)

Let us labour therefore (11) (But be ye doers of the word and not hearers only)

Let us therefore come boldly (16)

Jer 29:11 For I know the thoughts that I think toward you, saith the LORD, thoughts of peace, and not of evil, to give you an expected end.

Rom 8:37-39 Nay, in all these things we are more than conquerors through him that loved us. For I am persuaded, that neither death, nor life, nor angels, nor principalities, nor powers, nor things present, nor things to come, Nor height, nor depth, nor any other creature, shall be able to separate us from the love of God, which is in Christ Jesus our Lord.

2 Tim 1:12 For the which cause I also suffer these things: nevertheless I am not ashamed: for I know whom I have believed, and am persuaded that he is able to keep that which I have committed unto him against that day.

The answer to fear and failure is faith!

What word didn't they believe? The report of Joshua and Caleb – they chose to believe the majority report rather than the truth! Numbers 14:6-10

Verse 3

The saved have entered into the rest of the finished work of Jesus Christ. Jesus Christ was the Lamb of God slain before the foundation of the world and in God's eyes our salvation was and is complete. The saved are those who have fully trusted the finished work of Christ. Some are trying to be saved by Jesus plus their good works, their good deeds, their goodness, their church membership, their preaching, etc...

Eph 2:8-9 For by grace are ye saved through faith; and that not of yourselves: *it is* the gift of God: Not of works, lest any man should boast. Tit 3:5 Not by works of righteousness which we have done, but according to his mercy he saved us, by the washing of regeneration, and renewing of the Holy Ghost;

Verse 4-5

Creation Rest

God created everything that is created in 6 days and on the 7th day He rested.

Ge 2:1-2 Thus the heavens and the earth were finished, and all the host of them. And on the seventh day God ended his work which he had made; and he rested on the seventh day from all his work which he had made.

That doesn't mean that God wasn't doing anything, it means in relation to His work of creation, it was complete and He finished it.

Verse 6-8

Canaan Rest

(6) They could not enter in because of their unbelief, so God let them wander for 40 years until that unbelieving generation died off through attrition.

(7) Ps 95:7-8 For he *is* our God; and we *are* the people of his pasture, and the sheep of his hand. To day if ye will hear his

voice, Harden not your heart, as in the provocation, *and* as *in* the day of temptation in the wilderness:

(8) Jesus - Joshua. This happens 2x in NT; here and in Acts 7:44-47

Joshua - "a savior; a deliverer"

Jesus - "a Savior; a Deliverer" Matt 1:21 And she shall bring forth a son, and thou shalt call his name JESUS: for he shall save his people from their sins.

Joshua is a type of Jesus Christ....

Verse 9-11

Calvary Rest

(9) Future Rest –

(10) Finished Rest –

(11) Fighting Rest –

When the nation of Israel entered into the Promised Land, there were still enemies that they had to face and battles they had to win. When they followed the Lord in the battles, they were victorious! When they presumed upon the Lord and fought battles that God did not lead them into, they lost.

A dog can whip a skunk, but it just ain't worth it!

Acts 20:24 But none of these things move me, neither count I my life dear unto myself, so that I might finish my course with joy, and the ministry, which I have received of the Lord Jesus, to testify the gospel of the grace of God.

2 Tim 4:7 I have fought a good fight, I have finished *my* course, I have kept the faith:

How do we rest in the Lord?

1) Cease from our own works

Eph 2:10 For we are his workmanship, created in Christ Jesus unto good works, which God hath before ordained that we should walk in them. Php 1:6 Being confident of this very thing, that he which hath begun a good work in you will perform *it* until the day of Jesus Christ:

Remembering that we don't have to work to complete our salvation. We don't work to get saved; we work because we are saved.

2) Labour to enter His rest

Php 3:12-15 Not as though I had already attained, either were already perfect: but I follow after, if that I may apprehend that for which also I am apprehended of Christ Jesus. Brethren, I count not myself to have apprehended: but *this* one thing *I do*, forgetting those things which are behind, and reaching forth unto those things which are before, I press toward the mark for the prize of the high calling of God in Christ Jesus. Let us therefore, as many as be perfect, be thus minded: and if in any thing ye be otherwise minded, God shall reveal even this unto you.

Rom 12:1-2 I beseech you therefore, brethren, by the mercies of God, that ye present your bodies a living sacrifice, holy, acceptable unto God, *which is* your reasonable service. And be not conformed to this world: but be ye transformed by the renewing of your mind, that ye may prove what *is* that good, and acceptable, and perfect, will of God.

(ill) A missionary in Africa was riding down a road in his pickup truck. He came upon a native walking along the road, struggling with a heavy load on his back. The missionary offered him a ride in the back of his truck. The native got in gladly. After several miles, the missionary looked in the back and was surprised to see the African standing in the back of the truck with his heavy pack still strapped to his back. He stopped the truck and asked why. "I didn't think about it."

(ill) A man is swept out to sea in a raft with only one paddle. The waves beat against the raft, the winds blow, and all of the man's effort to bring him to shore are to no avail. He struggles, rows, sweats, works hard but his efforts are futile. Suddenly, beside him is the Old Ship of Zion. The crew throws him a line and bids him come aboard. He accepts the invitation and now stands on board, saved and safe! There is solid planking beneath his feet and roaring engines are taking him closer and closer to shore. He is taken to the Captain of the ship, who welcomes him aboard. Then the captain asks him to help out on the ship for they are seeking others lost at sea before they come to shore. "Will you help? If you refuse, you will not be cast back into the sea, but we sure could use your help". His salvation is secure, his helping out on board does nothing to make him more saved, but it helps other to be saved.

Verse 12-16
Resources to enable us to enter into His rest.
Holy pages of Scripture
High Priest, God's Son

Verse 12
Sharper than any two-edged sword...the Word of God is likened unto many things in Scripture...
Lu 8:11 Now the parable is this: The seed is the word of God.
Jer 23:29 *Is* not my word like as a fire? saith the LORD; and like a hammer *that* breaketh the rock in pieces?
Now, the writer of Hebrews likens it unto a two-edged sword.
Quick – "alive"
Eph 6:17 And take the helmet of salvation, and the sword of the Spirit, which is the word of God:
There is a difference between a physical sword and the sword of the spirit.
A physical sword stabs living people and makes them dead; the sword of the spirit stabs dead people and makes them alive.
Eph 2:1 And you *hath he quickened*, who were dead in trespasses and sins;
It is alive continually...
It is alive in every generation.
(ill) Martin Luther was a catholic monk. He began to study the book of Romans for himself. As he studied, the living Word of God became alive in his soul when he read, "The just shall live

by faith." He was climbing stone stairs on his hands and knees doing penance for his sins, and that Living Word quickened his dead spirit, and Martin Luther was transformed and became the great dark ages reformer.

The Bible is a living book because its Author and subject is the living Lord. it is like no other book that has ever been written. Every book has an author and every book's author is dead or will die. This book's author will never die.

John 6:63 It is the spirit that quickeneth; the flesh profiteth nothing: the words that I speak unto you, *they* are spirit, and *they* are life.

Powerful - Productive – it works in people's lives. No other transforming power can wash away sins, break hardened hearts, and convert rebels into redeemed saints but the Word of God.

1) It can cleanse - John 15:3 Now ye are clean through the word which I have spoken unto you.

2) It can comfort - Ps 119:50 This *is* my comfort in my affliction: for thy word hath quickened me.

3) It can conform - John 17:17 Sanctify them through thy truth: thy word is truth.

1 Thes 2:13 For this cause also thank we God without ceasing, because, when ye received the word of God which ye heard of us, ye received *it* not *as* the word of men, but as it is in truth, the word of God, which effectually worketh also in you that believe.

Piercing

(ill) Day of Pentecost, Peter stood up and preached the death, burial, and resurrection of Jesus Christ. Acts 2:37 Now when they heard *this*, they were pricked in their heart, and said unto Peter and to the rest of the apostles, Men *and* brethren, what shall we do?

(ill) Acts 16, Paul and Silas in prison praying and singing praises unto God.

Acts 16:29-31 Then he called for a light, and sprang in, and came trembling, and fell down before Paul and Silas, And brought

38

them out, and said, Sirs, what must I do to be saved? And they said, Believe on the Lord Jesus Christ, and thou shalt be saved, and thy house.

It goes deep – discerner of the thoughts and intents of the heart…
1) The Word of God EXAMINES our lives
People see what we do, God sees why we do what we do
2) The Word of God EXPOSES our lives
"I've read many books in my life, but this is the only Book that reads me."
This is the main reason people do not want this Book in their lives. They will settle for a substitute but not this Book.
(ill) Devil tempted Jesus in the wilderness 3x and every time Jesus quoted scripture.
Ps 149:6 *Let* the high *praises* of God *be* in their mouth, and a twoedged sword in their hand; Jer 48:10 Cursed *be* he that doeth the work of the LORD deceitfully, and cursed *be* he that keepeth back his sword from blood.

Quick – alive
Powerful – operative; active; effectual
Sharper – more keen, more effective; does not need to hack at its object
Piercing – to reach through; to cut to the base of
Discerner – one who sees and distinguishes; one who knows and judges
Intents – the stretching of the mind on a given subject; eagerly in pursuit of an object
Naked and Opened – to seize by the neck and expose the gullet of a victim

Verse 14
Hold Fast – to obtain and retain; to lay hands on and not let go
Profession – an open declaration; the business which one professes to understand and to follow for employment.

39

1 Tim 6:12 Fight the good fight of faith, lay hold on eternal life, whereunto thou art also called, and hast professed a good profession before many witnesses.

Verse 15
Touched – to have compassion on; to know what one is feeling;

Verse 16
Boldly – with confidence; assurance; plainly; openly
Since He already knows the truth about us, we might as well be truthful with Him about what is in our heart.
Heb 10:19-23
Jesus knows your: Name, Nature, Need
Matt 6:8 Be not ye therefore like unto them: for your Father knoweth what things ye have need of, before ye ask him.

CHAPTER 5

Remember that the writer of Hebrews is comparing OT to NT and the fact that Jesus Christ makes everything better. The word "better" is found 13 times in Hebrews. Better: Resurrection, Country, Things, Hope, Sacrifices, Promises, Covenant, Substance, Jesus is Better than anything or anyone!

Chapter 5 deals with the actual office of the high priest. In Hebrews the phrase "high priest" is found 16 times.

2:17; 3:1; 4:14; 4:15; 5:1; 5:5; 5:10; 6:20; 7:26; 8:1; 8:3; 9:7; 9:11; 9:25; 10:21; 13:11

While the gospels go into detail of the birth and life of Jesus Christ while He was upon earth, the book of Hebrews tells us what Jesus Christ is doing now that He has ascended back into Heaven to sit upon the right hand of God as the High Priest of the saved.

John 16:7 Nevertheless I tell you the truth; It is expedient for you that I go away: for if I go not away, the Comforter will not come unto you; but if I depart, I will send him unto you. (3:1; 4:14-16)

Verse 1–4

These verses describe the relationship, role, and responsibility of the EARTHLY high priest in the OT.

Verse 1

His RELATIONSHIP – a high priest represented man to God
The word "high priest" appears 80 times in the Bible in 77 verses.

Aaron was the first high priest and his sons were priests under him.

Exodus 28:1-3

Verse 2

Since the high priest was to represent the people that came before him, it was needful to select someone from among men in order for the representative to understand their needs.

Ignorant – "those that do not understand"

Have you ever read the laws that governed the sacrifices that the priests were to offer unto God?

Leviticus 1:2-13 There were sweet savor offerings; non-sweet savor offerings; burnt offerings; meal offerings; firstfruit offerings; peace offerings; meat offerings; sin offerings; trespass offerings; peace offerings and every offering had its own laws that governed the way that the offerings were to be presented to the Lord.

Out of the way – "those who have been deceived; those that have gone astray or out of the way"

Compassed – "bound; encircled; hampered; to be enclosed with"

Infirmities – "without strength; weakness; moral frailty; disease" it comes from the word in which we get our word anesthesia from. When you go under anesthesia, you are completely without strength and subject to whatever comes your way!

Verse 3

Leviticus 4:1-3

Verse 4

God was the One who chose the high priest, but even though God handpicked these men, they were sinners themselves. In the days of Jesus, the high priests were Annas and Caiaphas. They used their office for power and personal gain.

Verse 5

Establishing the groundwork for the earthly priesthood, the Hebrews' writer now moves to his intended subject Jesus Christ as our High Priest. He will compare the earthly high priest to our heavenly High Priest.

Jesus Christ did not glorify Himself as a High Priest, nor did He choose this office for Himself; it was entirely the decision of His Father.

While Jesus was on earth, He never served in the capacity of High Priest. His mission while on earth was predestined before the foundation of the world.

Rev 13:8 And all that dwell upon the earth shall worship him, whose names are not written in the book of life of the Lamb slain from the foundation of the world.

Philippians 2:5-11

John 8:54 Jesus answered, If I honour myself, my honour is nothing: it is my Father that honoureth me; of whom ye say, that he is your God:

Ps 2:1-7

What does it mean that God has "begotten" Jesus Christ? Jesus Christ never had a beginning; He is eternal God!

Acts 13:33

The word begotten means - "to bring forth; to spring up"

Acts 13:29-30

(ill) Larry King, unconverted Jew interviewed over 60,000 people in his lifetime. 7 presidents, world leaders, actors, actresses, authors, Martin Luther King, Nelson Mandella, always wanted to interview Castro but never did. He was asked the question one day, "If you could interview God, what would be the one question you would ask him?" His answer, "I would like to ask God, 'Did you really have a Son?' "

Verse 6

Ps 110:4-6

43

This High Priest after the order of Melchisedec, is coming back. He is seated right now, but He is going to get up one day and come back to this earth and rule this earth for 1,000 years.

Verse 7

Now the writer goes back to the time when Jesus was on earth because he wants us to understand something about our High Priest. Before He was a high priest, He prayed, made supplications with strong crying and tears, and He feared! Jesus Christ learned what it meant to have to completely depend on God being SUFFICIENT in death! God could not die; so He robed Himself in the likeness of sinful flesh to come into this world and experience death as man experiences it and depending completely upon God, His Father, to raise Him from the dead. Hebrews 2:14-18

Verse 8

Learned – "to gain knowledge of; to acquire knowledge or ideas of something before unknown. We learn the use of letters, the meaning of words and the principles of science. We learn things by instruction, by study, and by experience and observation."
Can you imagine God learning anything? The One who created everything and made everything perfect so much so that it baffles the minds of men so much that they cannot imagine a Creator and try to explain His handiwork away through the clap trap theory of evolution, learned!
Obedience – "to submit to; to conform to a command or authority"
Jesus had never been under the command of anyone or anything. He was God seated upon the throne of eternity commanding the sun to shine, the moon to reflect, the stars to twinkle, the angels to fly, the oceans to swell and recede! Now the Commander learns to be commanded. How?

By the things which he suffered – "to feel the passion; the emotion; the vexation; the sensation; to feel the pain"
God sent one man into this world without sin, but none without suffering.

Verse 9
Perfect – "complete"
Heb 2:10
Matt 5:48 Be ye therefore perfect, even as your Father which is in heaven is perfect. Jas 1:4 But let patience have *her* perfect work, that ye may be perfect and entire, wanting nothing. Php 3:15 Let us therefore, as many as be perfect, be thus minded: and if in any thing ye be otherwise minded, God shall reveal even this unto you.
Author – "one who produces; creates; or brings into being"
Heb 12:2 Looking unto Jesus the author and finisher of *our* faith; who for the joy that was set before him endured the cross, despising the shame, and is set down at the right hand of the throne of God.
An author is one who writes a book. He is the one who has Authored your life; He is writing your life's book!
Eternal Salvation – "forever; perpetual; everlasting"
There are some that believe that the book of Hebrews teaches that you can lose your salvation; but how can you lose something that is eternal?
John 3:15 That whosoever believeth in him should not perish, but have eternal life. Rom 5:21 That as sin hath reigned unto death, even so might grace reign through righteousness unto eternal life by Jesus Christ our Lord. Rom 6:23 For the wages of sin *is* death; but the gift of God *is* eternal life through Jesus Christ our Lord.
Obey – believing is the only work that God will recognize in our salvation
John 6:28-29, 47

Verse 10

While Jesus Christ was on earth, He could NOT be a high priest! The priesthood of the OT was to be of the tribe of Levi, and Jesus Christ was from the tribe of Judah! There is an eternal priesthood that was in existence long before God ever established the Levitical priesthood!

Verse 11

Dull – "sluggish; lazy; slothful"

Hearing - Amos 8:11 Behold, the days come, saith the Lord GOD, that I will send a famine in the land, not a famine of bread, nor a thirst for water, but of hearing the words of the LORD: Jer 6:10 To whom shall I speak, and give warning, that they may hear? behold, their ear *is* uncircumcised, and they cannot hearken: behold, the word of the LORD is unto them a reproach; they have no delight in it. Matt 13:15-16 For this people's heart is waxed gross, and *their* ears are dull of hearing, and their eyes they have closed; lest at any time they should see with *their* eyes, and hear with *their* ears, and should understand with *their* heart, and should be converted, and I should heal them. But blessed *are* your eyes, for they see: and your ears, for they hear.

We now live by faith, and it is so important that we have a daily diet of the Word of God to build our faith! Faith cometh by hearing
(ill) Bro. Tom Williams told the story of him and his wife going to Jerusalem and while there his wife developed a spinal meningitis that put her in a comma. They got her back to America, and she was in a hospital for months. He played scripture in her room so she could hear the Word of God. Months later she began recovering and even though she was like a child, she recovered and went to meetings with her husband.

Verse 12

Teachers – Study to learn, learn to live, and live to lead others in the way of truth.

(ill) First saved, working at RR and paid to study. Started learning and excited about learning the Word of God; I could not get enough. One day, Phillip asking me a question about marriage, divorce and I knew the answers. He was smoking, and it aggravated me, and I short answered him, "You've got a Bible study it yourself." Holy Ghost smote my heart. I'm not teaching you what I am showing you just for your knowledge, I'm teaching you to teach others, and if you don't, I'll quit teaching you.

We should not be the kind of Christians that when questioned about what we believe our answer is, "My preacher said." We should study to show ourselves approved unto God and be able to answer for ourselves.

1 Pet 3:15 But sanctify the Lord God in your hearts: and *be* ready always to *give* an answer to every man that asketh you a reason of the hope that is in you with meekness and fear:

Milk – 1 Pet 2:2-3

Meat – 1 Cor 3:1-3; John 6:27 We need a proper balance of milk and meat in our lives. (ill) Bro Glass, fix him a plate to eat and drink milk with his meal.

Verse 13

Unskillful – "inexperienced"

If all you live on is milk, it will hinder and hamper your Christian walk.

There are treasures in the Word of God
Proverbs 2:1-9

Verse 14

Full Age – progression in Christian growth

1 John 2:1; 1 John 2:12-14

Little children, young men, fathers

Senses – "organs of perception"

"Have you lost your senses?" When we become dull of hearing, we become dull in our discernment of right and wrong.

Exercised – "trained; practice"

Romans 5:1-5

Grace life is a life of: tribulations, patience, experience, hope, not ashamed, able to love God more and others more.

Discern – "judge; esteem"

The world cries "Judge not" it's the only Bible verse they know, and they use it to justify themselves and their sin.

Matt 7:1-5

1 Thes 5:21; 1 Cor 2:15; Rom 12:9; John 7:24; 1 Kings 3:9-10; Ezek 44:23; Mal 3:18;

Lk 12:54-57 "to distinguish; to separate; to discriminate; to see the difference between two or more things."

Lessons Learned:

1) Jesus Christ is a better high priest than Aaron and his descendants

2) Salvation is eternal through Jesus Christ

3) The Word of God aids us in discerning between good and evil

CHAPTER 6

Remember, there are three books of the Bible (Matthew, Acts, Hebrews) that are hard to understand and a lot of erroneous teaching comes from these books. (2 Tim 2:15)

There is a difference between OT and NT. In the book of Matthew − when you read you must understand that the events happening in Matthew are still under the OT law. (ill) Jesus telling the 10 lepers to go show themselves to the priest. Why? Jewish law

When did the NT actually begin? Heb 9:15-17

Acts – A transitional book actually coming from OT to NT; law to grace; salvation by the law to salvation by the finished work of Christ; salvation being conditional to salvation being eternal.

Hebrews – A book written to Jewish converts that is explaining the difference between the OT rituals and religion and Christianity! Christ being so much better than the law of Moses. The NT is so much better than the OT.

The passage we are about to study is one of those hard passages and one of my favorite to teach from.

Verse 1

First principles – "rudiments; the building blocks" First grade stuff.

Let us go on – the theme of Hebrews – don't stay on the milk, grow in the Lord.

Perfection – "maturity; completeness; fulfillment" NOT sinless perfection.

Matt 5:48; Heb 7:19; Heb 10:1-4, 14; Heb 13:20-21; Gal 3:3

God looks at our lives as FINISHED and COMPLETE; He sees the end result of our lives. We only see through a glass darkly now, but one day we will see what God saw.

(Refer back to 5:12) First principles – the basics of Christianity; NT

Repentance from dead works – turning from – to Acts 26:15-20; Titus 1:15-16

Faith – Eph 2:8-10; Heb 11:1-3 (ill) Science and God, "Go make your own dirt."

Verse 2

Baptisms – Eph 4:4-6 Baptize - "to immerse, submerge completely, to be totally placed inside or into"

1) Water baptism – water over a man is the picture of the wrath of God upon man; 1 Pet 3:20-21; Isaiah 54:8-9; Matt 28:19-20

2) Spirit – This is the ONE baptism of Eph 4. This is what literally happens when a person gets saved. This is the only baptism that saves a man.
1 Cor 12:12-14; Gal 3:24-27

3) Fire – Matt 3:11; Acts 1:4-5; Acts 11:15-16; 2 Thes 1:7-9; Ps 97:1-3; Ps 21:8-9

Laying Hands – reason for this, Num 8:9-11 to show the importance of being a minister to the congregation and to the individual priests. Acts 13:1-4

Resurrection – the gospel power…1 Cor 15:1-4; the importance to us 1 Cor 15:12-19 The resurrection not only gives us hope in this life but in the life which begins at death!

Eternal Judgment – There are no second chances once a person dies without Christ, their fate is forever sealed. Jude 5-7. When someone is placed on death row, their fate is sealed. Some try to escape, but in God's system it is maximum security with no parole board, no appeals, no defense lawyer, no leniency for good behavior, no retrial, mistrial, no new evidence, no plea bargain, no mercy…Luke 16

Verse 3

This will we do – what? Go onto perfection. If we desire the milk of the Word and learn these first principles and desire to grow and mature in our Christian life, God will allow or permit us the blessings of knowing Jesus Christ in a fuller more mature relationship. Phil 2:12-14

Verse 4

Impossible – dealing with an impossible situation
Enlightened - "made to see" (ill) Paul, Acts 9
Tasted - "experienced" 1 Pet 2:3; Heb 2:9
Heavenly gift - Rom 6:23; Jas 1:17 Every good gift and every perfect gift is from above, and cometh down from the Father of lights, with whom is no variableness, neither shadow of turning.
Partakers - "to take part; to be a partner; to share or participate" Eph 3:6; Col 1:12; Heb 3:1; Rom 8:8-9; John 14:16-17

Verse 5

Word of God – Jer 15:16 Thy words were found, and I did eat them; and thy word was unto me the joy and rejoicing of mine heart: for I am called by thy name, O LORD God of hosts. (ill) John 4:31-34 John 4:34 Jesus saith unto them, My meat is to do the will of him that sent me, and to finish his work.
Powers of the world to come – already covered that expression in Heb 2:5
(Only saved people are said to be partakers; nowhere are lost people ever said to be a partaker of anything in Christ)

Description of lost man – Eph 2:1-3, 11-13

Verse 6

Renew – "to restore to a former state after decay"
Repentance – "a change of mind; a reversal of decision"
Crucify afresh – "to recrucify"
Open shame – "public example or disgrace"
Jesus Christ will never suffer for our sins again – He was crucified ONCE! Heb 9:26, 28; 1 Pet 3:18

(Eternal Life) John 3:15-16; John 10:28-30; John 17:2; Rom 6:23; 1 Tim 6:12, 19; Titus 1:1-2; 1 John 2:25; 1 John 5:9-13; (Rejecting Everlasting Life) –John 5:24; John 3:36; Acts 13:46; Rev 21:8

Verse 7-8
Illustration: The earth and God sending the blessing of rain upon the entire earth. But two outcomes or differences are mentioned.
1) One received the blessing of God and brought forth fruit.
2) One rejected the blessing of God and was nigh cursing and cast to burn.
There are only two kinds of people in the world…the saved and the lost. No in-between.
One bears fruit because it responds to God and the other does not because it does not respond to God.
Mark 4:1-9, 13-20; Matt 7:15-20; Titus 1:15-16; Matt 3:10; Gal 5:22

Verse 9
Titus 2:11-14

Verse 10
1) One way you can tell you are saved (or tell if someone else is saved) is by their desire to be with and minister to other Christians.
1 John 3:13-16; 1 John 4:11, 19-21; John 13:34-35; 1 Cor 16:15
One of the things that accompany salvation is learning how to love each other. (ill) Job and his three friends
1 John 3:1-3
Matthew 5:43-48
2) Another thing that accompanies salvation is realizing that your life is not your own any longer and serving God.
Rom 12:1-2

(ill) The example, Jesus Christ, NEVERTHELESS not my will…
Eph 6:6 Not with eyeservice, as menpleasers; but as the servants of Christ, doing the will of God from the heart;
Col 4:12; 1 Pet 4:2

Verse 11

Finish till the end. Live this way until the end of your life. Always striving, always working, always loving…
1 Cor 15:58
Those that believe that you can lose your salvation – "Well, I'm just away from God right now in my life…" That does not EXEMPT them from accountability. VACANCY does not exempt you from ACCOUNTABILITY.
(ill) Some believe, "Since I wasn't at church this particular Sunday, I don't have to tithe my money that week."

Verse 12

Faith and Patience
Faith – Belief, to the point you live it. Faith produces works in your life.
James 2:14-20
Romans 1:17 – The just
Gal 3:11 - shall live
Heb 10:38 – by faith
Every trial, everything that we go through – it takes faith to make it through.
Mark 11:22 And Jesus answering saith unto them, Have faith in God.
Increase our faith – Luke 17:1-5
Faith that fails not – Luke 22:31-32
Gal 2:20
The word faith appears in the Bible 247 times and only two times in OT.

Our eternal life begins by faith and we continue to live by faith not sight, circumstances, feelings…faith.

2 Cor 1:24 Not for that we have dominion over your faith, but are helpers of your joy: for by faith ye stand. Php 1:25 And having this confidence, I know that I shall abide and continue with you all for your furtherance and joy of faith; 2 Thes 1:3 We are bound to thank God always for you, brethren, as it is meet, because that your faith groweth exceedingly, and the charity of every one of you all toward each other aboundeth;

2 Tim 4:7 I have fought a good fight, I have finished *my* course, I have kept the faith:

Patience – (1828) The suffering of afflictions, pain, toil, calamity, provocation or other evil, with a calm, unruffled temper; endurance without murmuring or fretfulness. (Phil 2:12-15) (Heb 10:36)

1) Be patient with God working in your life (eternal life)

Php 1:6 Being confident of this very thing, that he which hath begun a good work in you will perform *it* until the day of Jesus Christ:

Lu 8:15 But that on the good ground are they, which in an honest and good heart, having heard the word, keep *it*, and bring forth fruit with patience.

Rom 5:1-5 Some of the things we go through are simply God wanting to show you just how much He loves you.

Rom 12:12; 2 Cor 6:4; Col 1:10-11; 2 Thes 1:4; James 1:2-5; Jas 5:11 Behold, we count them happy which endure. Ye have heard of the patience of Job, and have seen the end of the Lord; that the Lord is very pitiful, and of tender mercy.

2) Doing right and suffering for it

1 Pet 2:19-23

3) With men

1 Thes 5:14-15 (ill) Matt 18:23-35

Rom 15:4-5 For whatsoever things were written aforetime were written for our learning, that we through patience and comfort of the scriptures might have hope. Now the God of patience and consolation grant you to be likeminded one toward another according to Christ Jesus:

Slothful vs Diligence - "lazy; sluggish" vs "speed; with the sense of being dispatched; haste; forwardness" Too many Christians have a reverse gear or no gear at all.
Php 3:13-14 Brethren, I count not myself to have apprehended: but *this* one thing *I do*, forgetting those things which are behind, and reaching forth unto those things which are before, I press toward the mark for the prize of the high calling of God in Christ Jesus. Prov 12:24 The hand of the diligent shall bear rule: but the slothful shall be under tribute. Prov 12:27 The slothful *man* roasteth not that which he took in hunting: but the substance of a diligent man *is* precious. Prov 18:9 He also that is slothful in his work is brother to him that is a great waster. Prov 21:25 The desire of the slothful killeth him; for his hands refuse to labour. (ill) Prov 24:30-34

Followers – "pursue; to obey; to observe; to practice; to embrace"
To be a good follower:
1) Disciplined – "and the disciples followed him" Prov 25:28 He that *hath* no rule over his own spirit *is like* a city *that is* broken down, *and* without walls.
2) Deny Yourself – "if any man follow me, let him deny himself" (ill) Marks of last days – men shall be lovers of their own selves
3) Desire Leadership – 1 Thes 1:6; 2 Thes 3:7; Heb 13:7
2 thoughts: 1) Choose your heroes well! 2) You will never be a good leader until you learn to follow.

Verse 13
Swear – "to promise by an oath; to affirm or utter a solemn declaration" God could not swear by anything greater than

himself, so he swore by himself! Isaiah 44:6-8 – "As I live" Num 14:21; Ezek 33:11; Rom 14:11 (only time used in NT)

We are told not to swear - Matt 5:34-37 But I say unto you, Swear not at all; neither by heaven; for it is God's throne: Nor by the earth; for it is his footstool: neither by Jerusalem; for it is the city of the great King. Neither shalt thou swear by thy head, because thou canst not make one hair white or black. But let your communication be, Yea, yea; Nay, nay: for whatsoever is more than these cometh of evil. Jas 5:12 But above all things, my brethren, swear not, neither by heaven, neither by the earth, neither by any other oath: but let your yea be yea; and *your* nay, nay; lest ye fall into condemnation.

But God can, and He is the only one that can!

Verse 14-15

Abraham was 75 years old when God called him out and made a promise to him; (Gen 12:1-4). Abraham was a sojourner for 24 years and at the age of 99, God appears to him and promises him a seed that would forever inherit the land (Gen 17:1-8).

Verse 16

Swear – "to take an oath and stand by it; to affirm a declaration" Num 30:2 If a man vow a vow unto the LORD, or swear an oath to bind his soul with a bond; he shall not break his word, he shall do according to all that proceedeth out of his mouth. Ecc 5:4-5 When thou vowest a vow unto God, defer not to pay it; for *he hath* no pleasure in fools: pay that which thou hast vowed. Better *is it* that thou shouldest not vow, than that thou shouldest vow and not pay.

(ill) Jephthah, Judges 11:30-34

Verse 17

Immutability – (Only time used in word of God) "unchangeable"

Man believes in unchanging laws – (ill) Laws of nature - Gravity; he believes that the law of gravity will cause things to plummet to the ground, so he invents a parachute.

"If God could change for the worse, He would cease to be God; if He could change for the better, He would not have been God in the first place." Jerry Vines

Mal 3:6 For I *am* the LORD, I change not; therefore ye sons of Jacob are not consumed.

Oath – (ill) When someone stands in a courtroom and takes an oath; two things are happening. They, by the means of speaking words make a vow but at the same time, the words they are speaking are being written down for an affirmation.

Imagine – that we had no written Word of God. All we had is what other people told us God said. But God, more willing to abundantly show us his unchanging promise, had what He said written down and preserved for us forever! Ps 12:6-7 The words of the LORD *are* pure words: *as* silver tried in a furnace of earth, purified seven times. Thou shalt keep them, O LORD, thou shalt preserve them from this generation for ever.

Verse 18

Two – Two unchanging things – 1) What God said 2) What God wrote

(ill) When we take a loan at a bank, they make us promise to pay them back with interest. They also make us write it down and put it on paper, so there will be no confusion or breaking of those vows.

2 Pet 1:15-21

Matt 24:35 Heaven and earth shall pass away, but my words shall not pass away.

Consolation – "comfort"

Fled for Refuge – (the Hebrews would understand exactly what the writer of Hebrews was referring to) In the book of Numbers and Joshua, there was a provision made for someone who had murdered someone unawares.

Num 35:15 These six cities shall be a refuge, *both* for the children of Israel, and for the stranger, and for the sojourner among them: that every one that killeth any person unawares may flee thither.

Remember, a murderer had no provision for forgiveness in the OT. A murderer was to be put to death. But if someone killed someone and it was not premeditated or they simply were not aware that they were guilty of killing a person, certain cities were assigned as a refuge for them to flee to and the congregation would judge whether they were guilty of premeditated murder or if it was an accident. If it was an accident, they would remain in the city of refuge and the avenger of blood could not touch him.

Lay Hold – "to be strengthened by and retained"
1 Tim 6:12, 19

Hope – "confident expectation" Col 1:5 For the hope which is laid up for you in heaven, whereof ye heard before in the word of the truth of the gospel; 1 Pet 1:3 Blessed *be* the God and Father of our Lord Jesus Christ, which according to his abundant mercy hath begotten us again unto a lively ("alive for a lifetime") hope by the resurrection of Jesus Christ from the dead, 1 Tim 1:1 Paul, an apostle of Jesus Christ by the commandment of God our Saviour, and Lord Jesus Christ, *which is* our hope; Tit 1:2 In hope of eternal life, which God, that cannot lie, promised before the world began;

"If you could lose your salvation, He loses more than you do; He loses His holy, sacred character."

Verse 19

Anchor – (1828) An iron instrument for holding a ship or other vessel at rest in water. It is a strong shank, with a ring at one end, to which a cable may be fastened; and with two arms and flukes at the other end, forming a suitable angle with the shank to enter the ground.

Interesting word picture; "A crooked or curved arm"

(ill) Out with a man, "Let the anchor out." He forgot to fasten it to the cleat.

Within the veil – an earthly anchor goes downward, but a heavenly anchor goes up.

(ill) Little boy built a kite, flew it and it soared so high you could not see it. A man came along, "What are you doing?" Flying a kite. "I don't see a kite. How do you know you are flying a kite?" I can't see it either, but I feel its tug.

The UPWARD pull.

Verse 20

Forerunner (only time used) – "a scout that goes ahead to prepare the way"

John 14:1-6

High Priest Forever – while in the city of refuge, the manslayer was safe from the avenger of blood as long as the high priest lived. When he died, he wasn't safe any longer.

(1 John 5:9-13)

CHAPTER 7

Paul has hinted at the subject of Melchisedec before in chapter 5, but his listeners were dull of hearing. Now Paul can't avoid the subject any longer. Paul has been itching to delve into the depths of Melchisedec, now he goes full steam ahead on this mysterious individual.

What Paul's intentions are, is to show the superiority of the priesthood order of Melchisedec verses the priesthood order of Levi.

A Jew would assume and be right that Jesus Christ could not serve as a priest while on earth because he was not of the tribe of Levi, but of Judah. A Jew would have a hard time reconciling and realizing that they did not need a "man priest" to represent them any longer before the presence of the Lord. Jesus is far superior to any earthly priest.

1 Tim 2:5-6 For *there is* one God, and one mediator between God and men, the man Christ Jesus; Who gave himself a ransom for all, to be testified in due time.

Verse 1

All we have recorded in the Word of God, before the Hebrews account concerning Melchisedec are three verses in Gen 14:18-20. Remember, Paul had been caught up into the third heaven and heard "unspeakable words, in which it is not lawful for a man to utter." Heavenly revelations were given to Paul, and he evidently tells us some of his revelations concerning Melchisedec.

King & Priest – under the OT, a king could not be a priest and a priest could not be a king. The two offices were entirely separate under the OT economy.

(ill) When King Uzziah went into the temple to offer sacrifices for himself, God struck him with leprosy.

Israel's kings descended from the tribe of Judah and the house of David; the priests, on the other hand, descended from the tribe of Levi and the house of Aaron. Melchisedec was a king/priest. As a king, he had power with men; as a priest, he had power with God.

Verse 2

King of Righteousness – the name Melchisedec means "king of righteousness or king of justice". The word Salem means, peace; Shalom. First; righteousness – after that peace. There is no peace without righteousness.

Isa 48:22 *There is* no peace, saith the LORD, unto the wicked.
Ps 85:10 Mercy and truth are met together; righteousness and peace have kissed *each other*.
(Kiss - "to fasten upon; to seize")
Rom 5:1 Therefore being justified by faith, we have peace with God through our Lord Jesus Christ:

Verse 3

Without - In the book of Genesis, (beginnings) there is no record of the parents, birth, lineage, death of this character Melchisedec.
He appeared suddenly, blessed Abraham and then disappeared.
The only other mention of Melchisedec is found in:
Ps 110:4 The LORD hath sworn, and will not repent, Thou *art* a priest for ever after the order of Melchizedek.
This is a prophetic utterance concerning Jesus Christ.
Made like the Son of God – Melchisedec is a type of Jesus Christ.
Who is this mysterious person? Some have conjectured that he was Shem, some say he was Enoch others summarize that he was a Christophany, meaning that this was an appearance of Jesus Christ before the incarnation.
(ill) "The angel of the Lord"; 4th man in the fire…

He was and is Melchisedec; the priest of the most high God

Verse 4

Melchisedec and Abraham partook of the Lord's supper together before the institution of the Lord's supper. Gen 14:18-20
Abraham gave Melchisedec tithes of everything he had gained in the spoil. Some argue that tithing is a matter of the law. Abraham tithed before the law.

Verse 5

Num 17 – Aaron's rod budded to show that it was the tribe of Levi that would be chosen to be a tribe of priests. Num 18:6-7 any stranger that tried to be a priest outside the tribe of Levi was to be put to death.
Tithing was instituted under the law and after the law.
Mal 3:8-11
2 Chr 31:5

Verse 6-7

In the OT, they tithed according to LAW. In the NT, we tithe according to LOVE! Under the OT, a man was considered a God robber if he did not tithe. Under the NT, a man shows God how much he loves his money or Jesus!
1 Cor 16:1-2
A tithe of the spoils…
If every child of God tithed according to the Word of God, the church would not need to beg for money. Tithing is God's way of taking care of His church and its ministries.
We should tithe because of the promises and blessings that God gives us!

Verse 8

God notices your tithe or lack thereof…
Mark 12:41-44

Verse 9-10

Levi payed tithes also…not even the preacher is exempt from paying tithes.

Verse 11

Perfection – maturity. What is the need of another priest if the Levitical priesthood was sufficient?

Verse 12

The Law – Acts 13:38-39; Rom 3:19-28; Rom 5:20; Rom 9:31-10:4; Gal 2:16; Gal 3:10-13, 21-25

The law EXCLUDED Jesus from being a priest. In the framework of the Jewish nation, there was the sense of superiority if you were from a certain tribe; especially the tribe of Levi.

Change in the law – the Jews had a hard time with this thought and this process…Acts 6:13-14; Rom 7:1-6 (When I visit someone in the hospital, I am not doing it to save myself or keep myself saved; I am fulfilling the royal law of Christ freely.)

New Law: John 13:34; James 2:8; Gal 6:2 – (ill) "Love one another" notes.

Verse 13

No one of the tribe of Judah offered anything at the altar.

Verse 14

Judah was the kingly tribe Ge 49:10 The sceptre shall not depart from Judah, nor a lawgiver from between his feet, until Shiloh come; and unto him *shall* the gathering of the people *be*.

Verse 15-17

John 10:16-18 the power of an endless life…Jesus lives.

When Jesus died on the cross, the veil in the temple was rent from top to bottom and for the first time in the history of the law abiding Jews, anyone could go directly into the Holy of Holies.

Verse 18-22
Now we have direct access unto God because of the fact that Jesus lives.

Verse 19
The law could mature no one. It was ritualistic, like a broken record. It was black and white. The moral laws of God still stand, but the ceremonial law of washing before you eat, keeping the candlestick burning, baking unleavened bread – is over!

Nothing Perfect – Heb 10:1-4; Ex 34:7

Better Hope – Eph 2:12 (Before we were saved, we had no hope; when I heard about the tribulation I was planning to enter in. When a Jew was under the law, he had no hope in that his salvation was entirely up to him and he had no hope of heaven.) John 14:15-18; Col 1:27; 1 Tim 1:1

Verse 20-21
We are secure not because of our promises, but the promises of God.

Titus 1:2

The priests of Aaron's order did not take the office of priesthood by oath. They were installed into those positions by heredity; but Jesus Christ was made a priest after the order of Melchisedec with an oath. Ps 110:4

Verse 22
Surety – "one who gives security for another" (ill) Bondsman, Job 9:32-33

Better testament – covenant

(ill) Song on radio, "I'm building a bridge to span the great divide. I received the plans from God. I'm making it sure and I'm making it wide. Somehow I'm going to make it, but the question is what about you?"

The word "testament" is not used in the OT. The first time it appears in the Word of God is found in Matt 26:28. (The word "remission" means to discharge or release, freedom or liberty of our sins.)

Jesus is the first one to use the word testament which means – "a contract or a covenant with a divisive will." (John 17)

The Old Testament demonstrates the HOLINESS of God in His Wrath! The NT demonstrates the HOLINESS of God in His Love! God tried to TELL the OT saints that He loved them (Jer 31:3), but in the NT God demonstrated His love toward us. Rom 5:8 But God commendeth his love toward us, in that, while we were yet sinners, Christ died for us. (Commendeth - "stand near and introduce oneself)

Verse 23-24

In the OT they were continually changing priests because of death. The new priest coming on board would have to be trained and then begin his experience of actually acting as priest on the behalf of the Jews. Our priest was trained, and He learned by experience what the needs of the NT saints are, and since He will never die He is able to represent us to God and God to us forever. We are saved by Eternal Life – 1 John 5:9-13

Heb 5:8-9 Though he were a Son, yet learned he obedience by the things which he suffered; And being made perfect, he became the author of eternal salvation unto all them that obey him;

Verse 25

Uttermost – "full or entirely"
2 Cor 1:8-10; Rom 8:26-30

We get the complete package.

By Him – John 14:6; Acts 13:38-39; 1 Pet 1:18-21. He is our High Priest and the ONLY High Priest.

Intercession – "to confer or entreat; to make a deal with" The only thing that pleased God who was angry with the wicked every day, was the sinless blood of Christ being applied to the mercy seat in heaven.

Luke 22:31-32 (Prayed - "to beg and bind oneself to that petition; to literally wrap himself around that prayer").

Verse 26

Holy – Divine in character

Harmless – innocent

Undefiled – pure

Separate from sinners – to excel beyond

Higher than the heavens – to be placed or esteemed higher than the abode of God. The main thing in heaven will not be heaven, but it will be Jesus!

Php 2:9 Wherefore God also hath highly exalted him, and given him a name which is above every name:

Verse 27

Offered up himself – 2 Cor 5:21 For he hath made him *to be* sin for us, who knew no sin; that we might be made the righteousness of God in him.

Verse 28

Consecrated – "devoted or dedicated to the service of God." We better thank the Lord in heaven for His faithfulness (dedication, consecration.)

Heb 13:5-6 (ill) Till The Storm Passes By Out on the waters storms raging high, the waters around them were trouble that night, fear filled their hearts they felt they would die, they failed to remember that the Master was nigh. He spoke the words and winds all stood still even the waters obey His will, He calmed their storm like He will mine, if I just remember He lives deep inside.

Chorus:
Why should I worry why should I fear, when the very same Jesus He stays always near, He lives in my heart and He hears when I cry, I'll call on His name till the storm passes by.

We read in the Bible when He walked with them, brought light to the darkness when the way grew dim, how great it would be to have His footsteps in mine, and walk with the Master all of the time, and when trials come and death seems so nigh, I'll call on the Master I know He'll get there on time, and when sickness comes and my body's in pain all I have to do is call on His name.

CHAPTER 8

There is a tendency for those who have come out of a "religion" of traditions, rites, ceremonies, and beliefs to cling to some of that structure when they come to Christ. Peter addressed this in 1 Pet 1:18-21 Forasmuch as ye know that ye were not redeemed with corruptible things, *as* silver and gold, from your vain conversation *received* by tradition from your fathers; But with the precious blood of Christ, as of a lamb without blemish and without spot: Who verily was foreordained before the foundation of the world, but was manifest in these last times for you, Who by him do believe in God, that raised him up from the dead, and gave him glory; that your faith and hope might be in God.

So all through the book of Hebrews we find the emphasis or theme question:

"Why would you want to go back to something so inferior to Jesus Christ?"

Verse 1

Remember, the gospels tell us what Jesus did while He was on earth. The book of Hebrews tells us what Jesus is doing while He is in heaven.

Right Hand – Where Jesus SITS. (ill) In OT the Jewish Supreme Court of moral issues was known as the Sanhedrin. The high priest presided over the court and when moral issues were heard for judgment, the case would be brought before the high priest to judge and rule. On either side of the high priest were scribes, one on the left hand and one on the right hand. If someone were guilty of a crime or some act of moral disobedience, the scribe on the left hand would record the verdict and the sentence would forever be written and on record. If someone were found innocent and no condemnation was

exacted, the scribe on the right hand would write their name and the terms of their acquittal would be forever recorded.
Matt 26:63-66; Mark 16:19; Acts 2:33; Rom 8:34; Eph 1:17-23; Col 3:1; Heb 10:12; Matt 25:34
When it talks about the right hand of God in the OT, it is a reference to Jesus Christ – Ps 118:14-17; Ps 44:3-4; Ps 89:13-16; Ps 98:1-2

Verse 2
Minister – "a servant to a given people"
The true tabernacle – in heaven is the true tabernacle. God did not get his ideas from us, but we got our ideas from Him! Doors, windows, thrones, wheels, foundations…all of these ideas came from God. So when Moses made the tabernacle, he was making a figure of something that already existed. Ex 25:8-9; Heb 8:5. So when you study the tabernacle of Moses you are studying truths about heaven.
3 compartments – the outer court, the holy place, the holy of holies.
The outer court – brazen altar, brazen laver - John 15:3 Now ye are clean through the word which I have spoken unto you. John 17:17 Sanctify them through thy truth: thy word is truth.
The holy place – golden candlestick, golden table of showbread, golden altar of incense
The holiest of all – a perfect cube (Trinity), golden ark and mercy seat
Now we know that there are 3 heavens – The tabernacle represented man's quest to seek God and fellowship with Him. 2 Cor 12:1-5

Verse 3
Offer – His blood
John 20:15-20, 24-29

Verse 4

Jesus is not a priest after the law. Remember the law excluded Jesus even though He fulfilled the law. Luke 17:14, Jesus told the 10 lepers to go show themselves to the priests to make an offering for their sins. In the gospels, when Jesus forgave someone, the basis for forgiveness was always – grace; never their sacrifice. (ill) "If I'll do something, Jesus will forgive me." All you have to do is ask! 1 John 1:4-10

Verse 5

While in the mount, God showed Moses the PATTERN - "to stamp a mark into or print; strike; scar; smite; wound". When God was showing Moses the pattern of the tabernacle, He was showing him what would eventually happen to Jesus on the cross. The tabernacle speaks of Jesus Christ in every detail.

Verse 6

Mediator – "one who interposes parties or individuals at variance or disagreement." A mediator MUST be able to well represent both parties at odds with each other. The purpose of a mediator is to bring the two into agreement with each other thereby making peace. Gal 3:19-20; 1 Tim 2:5-6; Job 9:32-33

Verse 7

The law is good. Rom 7:12-13; 1 Tim 1:5-11 BUT the law cannot save anyone because of our sinfulness. Gal 3:21-22; Rom 8:3

Verse 8

Fault with them – God found fault not just with the Jews but also the priests that handled the law and its ordinances.
New Covenant – Jer 31:31-34; Jer 23:5-8; Jer 30:3; Rom 11:25-32; Jer 30:10-11. This covenant will be made with the nation of Israel during the millennium reign of Christ.

Verse 10

After those days – the tribulation period, a time of purging and chastisement for the nation of Israel. Jer 30:5-7

Verse 11

Not teach – Zech 13:1-5

Verse 12

Jer 50:20

Vese 13

A new covenant – Many covenants found in the word of God.

The Bible Covenants – Dr. T. John Dell

1. A mutual consent or agreement of two or more persons, to do or to forbear some act or thing; a contract; stipulation. A covenant is created by deed in writing, sealed and executed; or it may be implied in the contract. (Web 1828)

1.   Adam's (Edenic) Covenant – Genesis 1:26-30; Genesis 2:15-17 CONDITIONAL

2.   Noah's (Everlasting) Covenant – Genesis 6:18-22; Genesis 9:8-17 UNCONDITIONAL

3.   Abraham's (Land) Covenant – Genesis 12:1-4; Genesis 13:14-18; Genesis 15:1-21 UNCONDITIONAL
        Passes down through the descendants of Abraham – Isaac – Jacob (Israel; Genesis 32:28)

a) Promises originally that Abram would become a great nation and people would be blessed through Abram or cursed depending on their treatment of Abram; Genesis 12:1-3. The main intent of this covenant is God's blessings upon man through Abram

b) The promise of land and Abram's (physical) seed (as the sand of the sea) would inherit this land; Genesis 13:14-18; Genesis 15:18-21

c) The promise also included a spiritual seed (as the stars of heaven, Genesis 15:5-6)

d) Sign of covenant – Circumcision; Genesis 17:9-14 CONDITIONAL (Any male not circumcised broke the covenant and would be cut off).

4. Moses' (Law) Covenant – Exodus 19:3-8 CONDITIONAL

a) Included 10 commandments

b) Included 613 commandments that dealt with marriage, sex, hygiene, diet, finance, welfare, government, political alliances, etc…

c) Included the tabernacle and sacrifices administered by the Levitical priests

d) Included the death penalty for murder, adultery, breaking the Sabbath, rebellion against parents, witchcraft and Spiritism, sexual perversion (including homosexuality and beastiality).

e) Israel was to be a holy nation (different from the other nations)

f) This covenant was conditional and temporary and everything fulfilled by Jesus Christ on the cross (Now, Jews do not have to keep the law for righteousness but they need to believe on Jesus Christ for salvation; Romans 10:1-13)

5.	David's (King) Covenant – 2 Samuel 7:12-17
	UNCONDITIONAL
	a)	Involved the kingly lineage
	b)	Included the sure mercies of God (2 Samuel 7:15; Isaiah 55:3)
	c)	Followed through to the Lord Jesus Christ (Matthew 1:1)
	d)	Will be fulfilled during the millennium (Luke 1:30-33)

6.	Jesus' (Eternal Life) Covenant – Titus 1:2; Revelation 13:8
	a)	Sealed by the blood of Christ (Matthew 26:28)
	b)	Offered freely to whosoever – CONDITIONAL (John 1:11-12; John 3:15, 18; 1 John 5:9-13)
	c)	Gift of eternal life (Romans 6:23)

7.	Israel's (New) Covenant – Hebrews 8:7-13

(We that are saved by grace do not need a new covenant, the one we are under is for eternity.)

The OT	The NT
Mediator – Moses	Mediator – Jesus
Conditional	Unconditional
Justification could not be obtained	Justification Imputed
Written on dead stones	Written in living stones

CHAPTER 9

Verse 1

Ordinance – "a rule established by authority; a sentence or formal decree"
The first time that the word is used in Bible is Ex 12:14
Ex 12:14 And this day shall be unto you for a memorial; and ye shall keep it a feast to the LORD throughout your generations; ye shall keep it a feast by an ordinance for ever.
Numbers 10 – Ordinance pertaining to blowing the trumpets
Numbers 18 – Ordinance concerning the heave offerings
Numbers 19 – Ordinance of the red heifer
Numbers 31 – Ordinances of war
Kings would make ordinances – 1 Sam 30:24-25 For who will hearken unto you in this matter? but as his part *is* that goeth down to the battle, so *shall* his part *be* that tarrieth by the stuff: they shall part alike. And it was *so* from that day forward, that he made it a statute and an ordinance for Israel unto this day. 2 Chr 2:4 Behold, I build an house to the name of the LORD my God, to dedicate *it* to him, *and* to burn before him sweet incense, and for the continual shewbread, and for the burnt offerings morning and evening, on the sabbaths, and on the new moons, and on the solemn feasts of the LORD our God. This *is an ordinance* for ever to Israel.

The church also has ordinances – 1 Cor 11:2 Now I praise you, brethren, that ye remember me in all things, and keep the ordinances, as I delivered *them* to you. The Lord's Supper and Baptism.

Divine Service – the service was divine, but the ordinances were carnal (verse 10) and the sanctuary was worldly. The sanctuary was in the world, it had ordinances carried out by carnal men, but the service was divine, in that it kept man right with God.

* Names of the Sanctuary:

The Tabernacle – Ex 25:9

The Sanctuary – Ex 25:8

The Tent of Testimony or Witness – Num 9:15, 17:7

The House of God – Ex 34:26; Deut 23:18

The Tent of the Congregation – Ex 40:34-35

* The Purpose of the sanctuary – Ex 25:8 that he might dwell with them

Dwelling places of God:

1) Garden of Eden – Gen 3:8, 24

2) Individually – Noah, Enoch, Abraham, Moses

3) The tabernacle of Moses – Ex 25:8, 22

4) The temple of Solomon – 2 Chr 5

5) Jesus Christ – John 1:14; John 2:19-22; 2 Cor 5:18-19

6) The believer – Col 1:27; 2 Cor 5:1; John 14:23 Our bodies called a tabernacle

7) The church – 1 Tim 3:15; Eph 2:19-22

8) New Jerusalem – Rev 21:3

* 7-fold requirement for building the sanctuary

1) By freewill offering – Ex 25:2

2) By a people stirred up – Ex 35:21, 26 you will give yourself to whatever stirs you

3) By a people made willing – Ex 35:5, 21-22, 29 "Lord, I'm willing for you to make me willing."

4) By a free hearted people – Ex 35-36 (Not complaining about it; Phil 2:12-15)

5) By the wisdom of God – Ex 36:1-8 If any man lack wisdom

6) By the Spirit of God – Ex 35:30-35 the Lord of the Harvest

7) According to the divine pattern – Ex 25:40; which is Jesus Christ

* The Result – Ex 40:33-38 till Christ be formed in you…

It took Moses and the workers approximately 9 months to build the tabernacle.

In the womb of the virgin Mary, it took 9 months to construct the body that God would inhabit in human form. #9 in Bible is the number of fruit…

* Materials Used –

Gold, silver, brass, precious stones, fine linen, shittim wood, oil for light, spices for the anointing oil, spices for sweet incense.

* Covering

Goats hair (sin);

Rams skin dyed red – sacrifice & substitution (ill) Abraham & Isaac, ram caught in a thicket

Badgers skin – On the outside ugly, unappealing to the eye – but on the inside was all gold and worth. Isa 53:2 For he shall grow up before him as a tender plant, and as a root out of a dry ground: he hath no form nor comeliness; and when we shall see him, *there is* no beauty that we should desire him.

*Colors

Blue – heaven

Purple – royalty

Scarlet – blood

1 Pet 2:9-10 But ye *are* a chosen generation, a royal priesthood, a holy nation, a peculiar people; that ye should shew forth the praises of him who hath called you out of darkness into his marvellous light: Which in time past *were* not a people, but *are* now the people of God: which had not obtained mercy, but now have obtained mercy.

Verse 2

The first – the holy place or the sanctuary. Candlestick, table of showbread. Altar of incense not mentioned

Verse 3

The Holist of all – where the presence of God was at. Could not see Him, but He was there.

Verse 4

Golden censer – used by the high priest when he went into the Holiest of all with the blood

Num 16:46 And Moses said unto Aaron, Take a censer, and put fire therein from off the altar, and put on incense, and go quickly unto the congregation, and make an atonement for them: for there is wrath gone out from the LORD; the plague is begun. Rev 8:4 And the smoke of the incense, *which came* with the prayers of the saints, ascended up before God out of the angel's hand.

You can't separate God and your prayers. Your prayers are being presented before an everlasting God. (ill) Saint of God, praying for years for the salvation of her wayward son, she dies. One day up in heaven an angel comes and tells her that Jesus would like to see her at the throne. There he lets her know that her prayers for her wayward son have been answered.

Ark of the covenant –

4 arks mentioned in Scripture – Noah's ark (PRESERVATION of God), the ark where the baby Moses' was laid (PROTECTION of God), the ark of the covenant (Pardon of God), the ark in heaven (PRESENCE of God, Rev 11:19).

Golden pot of manna - PROVISION of God (Physical needs)

Aaron's rod that budded - POWER of God (Spiritual needs)

Tables of the covenant - PROMISES of God – (Moral needs)

Heb 8:6 But now hath he obtained a more excellent ministry, by how much also he is the mediator of a better covenant, which was established upon better promises.

Verse 5

Cherubims of glory

PROCLAMATION of God. The cherubim represented every creature in the universe. 4 faces – Man (human beings); Ox (domesticated animal); Lion (wild animal); Eagle (flying animal). In the book of Revelation 4:6-8

All four faces constantly looked at the blood. All of creation is relying on the shed blood of Jesus Christ.

Rom 8:19-22 For the earnest expectation of the creature waiteth for the manifestation of the sons of God. For the creature was made subject to vanity, not willingly, but by reason of him who hath subjected *the same* in hope, Because the creature itself also shall be delivered from the bondage of corruption into the glorious liberty of the children of God. For we know that the whole creation groaneth and travaileth in pain together until now. Isa 11:6 The wolf also shall dwell with the lamb, and the leopard shall lie down with the kid; and the calf and the young lion and the fatling together; and a little child shall lead them. Isa 65:25 The wolf and the lamb shall feed together, and the lion shall eat straw like the bullock: and dust *shall be* the serpent's meat. They shall not hurt nor destroy in all my holy mountain, saith the LORD.

Why? Because the Lord is PITIFUL!

Isa 63:9 In all their affliction he was afflicted, and the angel of his presence saved them: in his love and in his pity he redeemed them; and he bare them, and carried them all the days of old. Jas 5:11 Behold, we count them happy which endure. Ye have heard of the patience of Job, and have seen the end of the Lord; that the Lord is very pitiful, and of tender mercy.

*** One creature not represented in the cherubim – reptile class – no serpent – no devil in heaven. Rev 20:10 And the devil that deceived them was cast into the lake of fire and brimstone, where the beast and the false prophet *are*, and shall be tormented day and night for ever and ever.

Mercy Seat - pardon of God

Verse 6

Service of God – letting the light shine, Word of God, prayer

Verse 7

The high priest – Sir Robert Anderson says in his book, *The Hebrews Epistle in the Light of the Types*:

"While the old covenant had an earthly sanctuary and a human priesthood, the sanctuary of the new covenant is heaven itself, and the Great Priest who ministers there is no other than the Son of God...So exclusive are the prerogatives of the sons of Aaron, that while on earth not even the Lord Jesus Christ could share them. What a staggering fact it is that, during His earthly ministry, the Son of God Himself could not pass within the veil which screened the antechamber to the holy shrine! The very existence of this antechamber - the "first tabernacle" of Hebrews – gave proof that "the way into the holiest of all was not yet made manifest."

Once every year – the day of atonement. Every year there was a reminder made of their sins. But Jesus died ONCE and for all eternity, never to remind you of your sins. Heb 9:26 For then must he often have suffered since the foundation of the world: but now once in the end of the world hath he appeared to put away sin by the sacrifice of himself.

Verse 8

The tabernacle veil also reminded them – they could not get to God.

Verse 9

Perfect – mature

Conscience – our conscience has a double function (accuse us or excuse us)

Rom 2:14-16 For when the Gentiles, which have not the law, do by nature the things contained in the law, these, having not the law, are a law unto themselves: Which shew the work of the law written in their hearts, their conscience also bearing witness, and *their* thoughts the mean while accusing or else excusing one another. In the day when God shall judge the secrets of men by Jesus Christ according to my gospel.

The only people that have a clear conscience, a purged conscience – the child of God whose conscience has been purged by the blood!

Heb 9:14

Verse 10

Imposed – laid upon; pressed upon; "to burden with as a duty or penalty"

Reformation – (only time used in Bible) to straighten out thoroughly; "to correct or amend life, manners or anything that is vicious or corrupt"

Also called Regeneration – Matt 19:28

Or the Times of Refreshing & Restitution – Acts 3:19-21

Verse 11

Remember, the veil kept all Jews except one away from the presence of God. Only one man (the high priest) was ever qualified or allowed to enter into the Holy of Holies and the only time that he could enter in was once a year during the feast of atonement. Every other human being, including Gentiles, was omitted from getting to God. The law was good but weak because of the sinful nature of man. The tabernacle was inadequate, in that it was only temporary and restrictive. The only thing that the tabernacle of Moses accomplished was to allow God to dwell with His people. All the ceremonies and ordinances were shadows and typified Jesus Himself and what He would accomplish on the cross of Calvary.

But Christ – the objective of Hebrews is to point Jewish converts to the SUPREMACY and SACRIFICE of Jesus Christ. This phrase appears 5x in scripture

2 Cor 4:5 For we preach not ourselves, but Christ Jesus the Lord; and ourselves your servants for Jesus' sake.

Gal 2:20 I am crucified with Christ: nevertheless I live; yet not I, but Christ liveth in me: and the life which I now live in the flesh I live by the faith of the Son of God, who loved me, and gave himself for me.

Col 3:11 Where there is neither Greek nor Jew, circumcision nor uncircumcision, Barbarian, Scythian, bond *nor* free: but Christ *is* all, and in all.

Heb 3:6 But Christ as a son over his own house; whose house are we, if we hold fast the confidence and the rejoicing of the hope firm unto the end.

Verse 12

The tabernacle of heaven is greater because:

1) It is Served by a Greater Priest
2) It is Situated in a Greater Place
3) It is Secured by a Greater Price

(ill) The OT was secured by the blood of animals, but now the blood of God's own Son secures our salvation. After the Civil War, many southern banks still accepted Confederate notes as currency (current) payment. But now, Confederate money will not redeem anything. Not worth anything except for museums or collectors but actual redemption – worthless. The blood of animals is now worthless because of the superior, sufficient blood of Christ.

Redemption - A.) Repurchase of captured goods or prisoners; the act of procuring the deliverance of persons or things from the possession and power of captors by the payment of an equivalent; ransom; release; as the redemption of prisoners taken in war; the redemption of a ship and cargo.

B.) Deliverance from bondage, distress, or from liability to any evil or forfeiture, either by money, labor or other means.

The blood of animals was insufficient for an eternal work to be done. All animals die. But Christ's blood was eternal blood and everything connected or touched by His blood is eternal.

(Covenant) Heb 13:20 Now the God of peace, that brought again from the dead our Lord Jesus, that great shepherd of the sheep, through the blood of the everlasting covenant,

(Redemption) Hebrews 9:12

(Us) John 6:54 Whoso eateth my flesh, and drinketh my blood, hath eternal life; and I will raise him up at the last day.

4) It is Supported by a Greater Plan – He entered once and for all.

With the death, burial, resurrection, and ascension of Christ back into heaven the entire religious system of the OT is obsolete.

Verse 13

The blood of bulls and goats was limited to Jewish believers who broke the 613 laws of God. Death was everywhere! Jewish believers were constantly bringing sacrifices to the priests to provide cleansing of their sins, but every time another sin was committed, they were reminded that they had to do something to satisfy God's law demand.

Verse 14

But now the shed blood of Christ does not constantly remind us of our sins, but it purges our conscience from dead works to serve the living God!

The blood of Christ does not remind us that we need to do anything – it reminds us that Christ has already done everything!!!

(ill) I'm saved and secured by Christ's shed blood! The Trinity in covenant with each other, allowing a sinner to enter this covenant forever.

John 10:27-30 My sheep hear my voice, and I know them, and they follow me: And I give unto them eternal life; and they shall never perish, neither shall any *man* pluck them out of my hand. My Father, which gave *them* me, is greater than all; and no *man* is able to pluck *them* out of my Father's hand. I and *my* Father are one.

Purge - "to cleanse or purify by separating and carrying off whatever is impure; to clear and cleanse from defilement"

From, To Serve – dead works; working for a hole in the ground. Working for a grave.

Eph 2:10 For we are his workmanship, created in Christ Jesus unto good works, which God hath before ordained that we should walk in them.

Matt 5:16 Let your light so shine before men, that they may see your good works, and glorify your Father which is in heaven.

2 Tim 3:16-17 All scripture *is* given by inspiration of God, and *is* profitable for doctrine, for reproof, for correction, for instruction in righteousness: That the man of God may be perfect, throughly furnished unto all good works.

Tit 2:13-14 Looking for that blessed hope, and the glorious appearing of the great God and our Saviour Jesus Christ; Who gave himself for us, that he might redeem us from all iniquity, and purify unto himself a peculiar people, zealous of good works.

Tit 3:8 *This is* a faithful saying, and these things I will that thou affirm constantly, that they which have believed in God might be careful to maintain good works. These things are good and profitable unto men.

Heb 10:24 And let us consider one another to provoke unto love and to good works:

Tit 1:15-16 Unto the pure all things *are* pure: but unto them that are defiled and unbelieving *is* nothing pure; but even their mind and conscience is defiled. They profess that they know God; but in works they deny *him*, being abominable, and disobedient, and unto every good work reprobate.

We are redeemed to serve!

(ill) A man I knew had this on his Bible – "Once saved; always serving"

Verse 15

Mediator – a go-between; a reconciler; (1828) one that interposes between parties at variance for the purpose of reconciling them to each other.

Job 9:1-4; 32-35

The Gentiles got in because the Jews rejected the Trinity. OT – they rejected God the Father; Gospels – they rejected God the Son; Acts 7 – they rejected the Holy Ghost and the gospel went out to the Gentiles. Because the OT Tabernacle and its sacrifices were insufficient no one in the OT had eternal life. But by the death of Christ the ones that were saved by means of the first testament, inherit eternal life and they could then enter heaven! No one in OT went to heaven when they died. They went to a place called death or as some refer to it, "Abraham's bosom".

(ill) Luke 15

(ill) Under the OT, the believer was bound by an enormous weight of debt he owed for his sins. The blood of bulls and goats only temporarily gave them forgiveness but it never cleared them of their debt of sin. The animals had no will in the matter, they were slain by the law. But Jesus Christ willed Himself to the cross.

Php 2:8 And being found in fashion as a man, he humbled himself, and became obedient unto death, even the death of the cross.

Ex 34:6-7 And the LORD passed by before him, and proclaimed, The LORD, The LORD God, merciful and gracious, longsuffering, and abundant in goodness and truth, Keeping mercy for thousands, forgiving iniquity and transgression and sin, and that will by no means clear *the guilty*; visiting the iniquity of the fathers upon the children, and upon the children's children, unto the third and to the fourth *generation*.

The blood of Jesus Christ reached as far back as anyone under the OT and granted them eternal life. The blood of Jesus Christ reached into the present of any believer and proclaims him justified! And the blood of Jesus Christ reaches into our future and secures us forever!

Verse 16

Testator – (1828) "a man who makes and leaves a will or testament at death"
John 19:30
The Last Will and Testament of Jesus Christ – John 17
At least 4 persons are involved in a last will and testament:
1) The Testator – the one making the will
2) The Heir – the one(s) who are the beneficiaries of the will
3) The Executor – the one appointed by the testator to carry out the terms of the will
4) A Witness - Witnessed by His Father
Heb 1:2; Gal 4:6-7; Rom 8:16-17
In the Last Will and Testament of Jesus Christ it is recorded that whosoever believes in Him will receive everything contained in the will.
All believers get it all!
(ill) Two bums who were lying around one day and one of them began crying. The other asked him what was he crying about. He responded, "I just found out that Rockefeller died." The other said, "Why are you crying, you weren't kin to Rockefeller." "I know, that's why I'm crying," he answered.
(ill) A man and his son spent their lives collecting rare paintings. The son was tragically killed and the father mourned and eventually decided to sell all of his paintings. The public was invited to the auction. On the day several millionaires and billionaires gathered to view and buy certain paintings that the collector had. When the auction began the auctioneer announced that the first painting was a portrait of the collector's son. No one was interested in the painting and the room was silent as the auctioneer opened the floor for bidding. The auctioneer stated that they could go no further until the portrait of the father's son was bought. Finally, one man in the room made a bid, the only

bid and the gavel hammered sold. Then the auctioneer announced to the crowd that the auction was now over and the gentleman who bought the portrait of the son would be awarded all the other paintings within the collection. "That's outrageous," shouted the crowd! No sir, "Whoever gets the son, gets everything."

Verse 18

Now comparing the first testament with the second, he makes mention that blood is what sealed the authenticity of the first. Usually, wills are made and confirmed with the signature of the testator. But God signed His will with blood.

Verse 19-21

Enjoined – (1828) "to order or direct with urgency; to admonish or instruct with authority; to command"
The blood shed in the OT was the blood of animals. The law was the will and it was conditional. When someone in the OT sinned, they had to bring an innocent animal to make an offering for their sin. The animals had no will in the matter, they were slain by the LAW. But Jesus Christ willed Himself to the cross. He was slain by LOVE.
Php 2:8 And being found in fashion as a man, he humbled himself, and became obedient unto death, even the death of the cross.

Verse 22

Almost all things – a sin offering required blood to be shed by an innocent animal. But if someone were too poor to bring an animal an offering of flour would be accepted. Also, not all sins had means of forgiveness…ie. Adultery, witchcraft, rebellion in a child…these were to be stoned to death. No forgiveness offered.

Verse 23

With these? – the blood

Better sacrifices – the body and blood of Jesus Christ

Verse 24

For us – we have a representative in heaven. Sometimes wills are contested and someone will claim that they have rights to the will even though the will excludes them. Clever attorneys can twist and completely annul the intended clauses in the will. The only true way to resolve any disputes would be for the dead testator to relive and declare his precise intentions, which would be an impossibility. But that is exactly what Christ has done; that is why He is both testator and mediator – it is all for us!

Verse 25-26

The OT high priest would have to appear once every year to atone for the sins of the nation of Israel. But Jesus has appeared once in the past (Calvary) to put away our sins. He is appearing now on our behalf as our mediator. The age of the law continued for 1500 years and a lot of blood was shed.

Verse 27-28

Once – (2x) Man dies once and then must face judgment; so Christ could only die once and only one time bear the penalty of our sins.

Jesus had a past appearing to REDEEM SINNERS, a present appearing to REPRESENT SAINTS and praise God a future appearing RESCUE THE SAVED!

CHAPTER 10

Verse 1-4

Shadow – A shadow is merely an outline of an object, not the object. A shadow declares that there is a real object there, but a shadow just outlines that object. Your shadow is an outline of you, but it is not you. It indicates that there is a "you," but it's not you. The shadow of a key cannot unlock a door. The shadow of food cannot feed a person. The shadow of Calvary could not do the work for sin that needed to be done.

The shadow of good things to come - could never satisfy the demands of God nor could they purge the sinner. The shadow only allowed them to stand with a reminder that there had to be something better. The shadow was not the real thing. A shadow cannot affect you. The law, the sacrifices, the ordinances were just the shadow of Jesus Christ. A shadow is always the same, one color – black, it never changes.

Repetitive, redundant, reminding; this is the summation of the OT. It was always reminding the sinner that they were a sinner. Nothing was ever finalized.

Ex 34:5-7 no clearing or purging of their sin.

All through the OT there was only the repetition of the signing of promissory notes. The blood that was shed for sin was good only until the next sin was committed; then blood had to be shed again. They were not able to pay their debt. It was never ending. "There's Got to Be Something Better"

Verses 5-10

Body - When Jesus came into the world, a body was prepared for Him. Before He came, He existed.

John 1:1-2, 14; Is 9:6; Rom 8:3

Pleasure – "to think well of; to approve" It was "thumbs down" in the OT. God had a better PLAN and PROVISION.

Verses 8-9

When God said, "I find no pleasure in the OT;" Jesus said, "Here I go to do Your will."

Establish – "to positionally apply and ordain"

Verse 10

Will – The will of Jesus Christ - John 4:32 But he said unto them, I have meat to eat that ye know not of. John 4:34 Jesus saith unto them, My meat is to do the will of him that sent me, and to finish his work. Lu 22:42 Saying, Father, if thou be willing, remove this cup from me: nevertheless not my will, but thine, be done.

Sanctified – "made holy"

Once and for all – We are out of debt spiritually

(ill) Suppose you owed a debt. You go to the bank to borrow money to pay the debt. They loan you the money on a 12 month note and you go pay your debt. Are you out of debt? No you still owe money (that is why borrowing money never frees you financially). At the end of the twelve months, you do not have the money to pay the debt, so you return to the bank and ask for an extension of your indebtedness. Now, instead of the original amount of debt you owe interest from the previous 12 months and are going to add more debt when you sign that note. Your debt is getting larger and larger. Suppose again that you did not know it, but you had a friend and this friend was super wealthy. You were talking to him one day and told him what a mess you had made of your life. After listening to your dilemma, your friend says, "I'll go to the bank and pay your debt for you. I'll pay it in full so that you will be totally out of debt." That is what Jesus did for us. We owed a debt morally and our indebtedness was growing every day. One day Jesus came along and paid our debt in full. We no longer owe for our debt. We are debt free. That's why when someone that has been under that sin debt load for years gets saved, they feel like a load has been lifted. That is also why God blesses anyone that desires to get out of debt and commits to never go in debt again. It is a reflection of what God has done for us spiritually!

Verse 11-12

Alluding to the fact that the OT priest had to continue offering, the writer then points us to Jesus!

One sacrifice was all that it took. He is now sitting down. He is not pacing the floor, ONE OFFERING DID THE JOB FOR EVER!

Verse 13

Enemies – Colossians 2:13-15 Our sins; the law; devils. Hebrews 2:14 the devil. 1 Cor 15:25-26 Death

Verse 14

Perfected – "completely matured or finished" YOU

Sanctified – "made holy and set apart"

That is what the world hates about Christianity; it sets us apart or differentiates us from all others. They will join a religion and become different because it is a change designed and established by man. But when it comes to us saying that God has made a difference in us – they will balk and criticize us for claiming that. Our change dealt with the root of the problem – our sinful nature. Their religion and even the OT ordinances could not get to the root of the problem.

Verse 15

Witness - Rom 8:16 The Spirit itself beareth witness with our spirit, that we are the children of God:

Verse 16

Covenant – the Trinity made a covenant with each other and we get inside that covenant.

He is referencing Heb 8:10

Verse 17

Remember – remembrance is a powerful thing. The dying thief cried on his cross, "Remember me." Verily I say unto you, Today thou shalt be with me in paradise. Why? Jesus has CHOSEN to remember us and forget our sins.

Verse 18

Remission – "freedom; deliverance; liberty" Liberty from sin...Rom 6:17-19
Gal 5:1 Stand fast therefore in the liberty wherewith Christ hath made us free, and be not entangled again with the yoke of bondage.

Verse 19

Boldness – "frankness; confidence; freeness; assurance"
Holiest – where God is seated – throne. Every time we pray, we are entering into a throne room where a king reigns. The same king that Abraham bowed before, Isaiah, Jeremiah, Daniel...but the difference now is that I have boldness to enter into that throne room because of what Jesus has done for me, not what I have done or not done. I enter into the presence of God based on the merits of the blood of the Son of God.
The NT believer is invited to do something only the high priest of the OT was allowed to do! Heb 4:15-16
(ill) Moabite walks up to the linen wall that shuts him out from the OT tabernacle and walks around to the eastern gate. A gate keeper is standing there and the Moabite enquires of what is going on inside. People are worshipping God in there! Can I go in? No you are an outsider, outside the commonwealth of Israel, you may not ever go in. The law of Moses has barred any Moabite from entering into the congregation of Israel. The Moabite asks what he would have to do to be allowed entrance in. The Jewish man informs him that the only way for him to enter would be a miracle in itself, and he would have to be born

again. Your first birth forbids entrance but if you could somehow enter the second time; not into the same womb but a totally different womb – a Jewish womb, and be born again of different stock, you would then be allowed to enter into the worship of God. What's in there? The tabernacle proper is there and the presence of God is in the tabernacle. Can anyone go where God is? Oh no, only the high priest is allowed entrance into the very presence of God. The Moabite says that if he were a high priest, he would go into the place where God is several times a day just to be able to enter into the presence of the living God. No you would not be allowed there either. The high priest is only allowed to go in there once a year, and that for only a short time. Sadly, the Moabite walks away without hope of ever getting to God; no hope of entering in.

Eph 2:11-18; 1 Pet 2:9-10

The PLACE of Access – the holiest

The PRICE of Access – the blood of Christ

The POSTURE of Access – boldness

The PROOF of Access – full assurance of Faith

The PERSON of Access – having a high priest

Verse 20

Consecrated – "dedicated; devoted" The throne room is always available. Every time an OT Jew needed forgiveness, he had to go round up the acceptable sacrifice and then make his way to the brazen altar. Hideous sight, blood all around the altar, flames blazing through the grating, and the smell had to be terrible. But we have a new and living way, and we can enter the throne room anytime, anywhere, about anything.

Verse 21

The high priest is always waiting on us, alive and well and willing to listen to our every cause. Our high priest did what no

OT high priest ever dared to do. He sat down inside the Holiest and bid others to come inside where He is.

Verse 22

Let us – One of 12 "let us" in the book of Hebrews.
4:1 – Let us therefore fear
4:11 – Let us labor therefore to enter into that rest
4:14 – Let us hold fast our profession
4:16 – Let us therefore come boldly unto the throne of grace
6:1 – Let us go on unto perfection
10:22 – Let us draw near with a true heart
10:23 – Let us hold fast our profession of faith
10:24 – Let us consider one another
12:1 – Let us lay aside every weight
12:1 – Let us run with patience
12:28 – Let us have grace
13:13 – Let us go forth therefore unto him without the camp
13:15 – Let us offer the sacrifice of praise to God continually
We can have a full head of "let us" because of Jesus Christ our Lord

Spiritual and physical cleanliness – "cleanliness is next to godliness." God wants you to take a bath; a physical bath and spiritual bath are similar.
(ill) As a little boy I loved to play outside. Come in, mom would tell me to go get my bath, and bathe all over. "Get behind your ears!" I would go in the bathroom, run some water, and pretend to bathe, put on my PJs and run tell mom I was clean. She would smell me and send me back; I could not fool mama. She could smell dirt. She used to tell me that I could grow corn at the foot of my bed there would be so much dirt under my sheets.
When you take a bath 1) you put off the dirty clothes, 2) you cleanse yourself 3) you put on new clothes or fresh clothes.
Eph 4:17-24; Col 3:8-13
1) Discarding of the Corruption

2) Deliberate Cleansing of the mind

Rom 12:2 And be not conformed to this world: but be ye transformed by the renewing of your mind, that ye may prove what *is* that good, and acceptable, and perfect, will of God.

3) Displaying of Christ

When God smells your life (and He did say that they were a sweet smelling savor unto Him) He will not smell the old dirt but smell the new man.

Verse 23

Maintenance is necessary. You do not take only one bath in life, we take many; some days, it is necessary to take several.

Verse 24

You have to do verses 22 and 23 before you can do verse 24.

1 John 1:8-10 these verses are necessary to maintain the fellowship with others in verses 3 & 6 and retain the joy of our salvation – verse 4.

Neh 8:10 Then he said unto them, Go your way, eat the fat, and drink the sweet, and send portions unto them for whom nothing is prepared: for *this* day *is* holy unto our Lord: neither be ye sorry; for the joy of the LORD is your strength.

Provoke - "to call into action; to arouse; to excite; to challenge…

1 Thes 4:9 But as touching brotherly love ye need not that I write unto you: for ye yourselves are taught of God to love one another. (1 John 4:19-21)

Verse 25

We need each other more as we see the coming of the Lord draw nigh. Loners will lose in the last days. There is strength in numbers and if you are going to be faithful unto the end, you will need the people of God around your life.

Faith is mentioned in this passage twice and catapults our faith against the faithfulness of Christ. Faith is important in our lives – Luke 18:1-8

The whole of the next chapter is entirely about faith, giving us a cloud of witnesses to the importance of faith in our lives.

(ill) Burning embers in a fireplace…preacher visiting a member that had grown cold on God and quit going to church. Winter time, entered into his house, had a roaring fire going in the fireplace. The two talked, the preacher noticed a burning ember fall and roll a little way from the fire and the rest of the embers. He reached with a fire poke and pulled the low glowing ember off to one side and let it sit there by itself and the fire went out in that ember. Then the preacher pushed the ember back into the heap with the rest of the embers and it started glowing again.

Verse 26

This is the 4th of 5 Warning Passages found in Hebrews.

1) 2:1-4 – Disregarding the Salvation of the Lord
2) 3:1-4:11 – Disbelieving the Sufficiency of God
3) 6:1-20 – Discrediting the Steadfastness of God
4) Text – Despising the Son of God

In light of all that has been said, the writer now turns his attention to those who have heard everything needed to lead them to a saving knowledge of Jesus Christ but are still about to turn away. In spite of everything, they are looking back to a dead religion. The warning placed before us is the strongest in the epistle. It has everything to do with DESPISING the Spirit of God and the consequences are clearly laid out.

Sin willfully – "a deliberate action; a deliberate sin; to volunteer". This is not a sudden impulsive decision but a settled resolve and intention of turning away from the ONLY WAY of salvation. There is no other sacrifice out there that God will accept EXCEPT the sacrifice of God's only Son, Jesus Christ.

Knowledge of the truth – 1 Timothy 2:3-4; 2 Thes 2:9-12; 2 Tim 3:1-7

John 14:6 Jesus saith unto him, I am the way, the truth, and the life: no man cometh unto the Father, but by me.

1) A DELIBERATE SIN

Verse 27

2) A DEVOURING SIN

There is no Limbo, Leniency, or Love of God involved in the pronouncement of judgment upon the damned. The closest a lost person will ever come to the love of God is while they are living upon earth. When they cross that line and pass into eternity without Jesus Christ – weeping, wailing and gnashing of their teeth.

Devour - "to eat away at; slowly but surely"

Adversary - "an opponent; one contrary or against"

(ill) The context concerns itself with how a generation handles truth; or how they respond to truth. Romans 1:16-32

Verse 28

Under the law, the despisers received no mercy! God's law said no adultery, and those that despised that law – died without mercy!

Despise - "to reject; to disesteem; to set aside; to cast off (1828) to scorn; to abhor"

Died without mercy – Mercy - "that benevolence, mildness or tenderness of heart which disposes a person to overlook injuries, or to treat an offender better than he deserves; to forbear punishment, or inflict less than law or justice will warrant."

(ill) Luke 16:19-26 – a place of no mercy

3) A DAMNING SIN

Verse 29

Despite - "angry hatred; violent anger"

Psalm 2

Verse 30

Deut 32:35 To me *belongeth* vengeance, and recompence; their foot shall slide in *due* time: for the day of their calamity *is* at hand, and the things that shall come upon them make haste.

4) A DONE SIN

Once it is done; God will have the upper hand and no one can reverse it.

Prov 1:24-30

Verse 31

5) The DEVIL'S SIN

Revelation 20:7-15

Verse 32-33

The writer of Hebrews has interjected a warning passage (26-31) in this chapter because he is writing to Jewish believers. A Jewish person who converted to Christianity was considered a traitor, a reprobate, and by his own family would be considered dead. There was and is even today much persecution among Jews who bow to Jesus Christ. There is much opposition among the Jews to keep any of their own from believing in Jesus Christ. Once someone of the Jewish race gets saved they are constantly accosted for their belief in Jesus. So the warning passage serves a two-fold purpose: 1) to warn any reader who might read this passage and 2) to comfort and encourage any believer who might be suffering by the unbelieving crowd.

Remember – the past. Do you remember when? You may not remember the date, but you remember there was a day when you got saved.

Illuminated – (only time used in Word of God) "to adorn with festive lights or bonfires; to enlighten intellectually with knowledge or grace; to illustrate or throw light on obscure objects.

2 Cor 4:3-4; 2 Cor 3:12-16;

(ill) John 9:25

Gazingstock – (only time used in Word of God) We get our word theatre from this Greek word (theatrizo) "to be placed for public show; to be set in a public show room" The devil will try to shame you before your family, friends…but God puts you on display to show this world – it is real!

(ill) The 1st century Christians were taken to the Roman coliseum and martyred for their faith by throwing them to the lions. *Foxes Book of Martyrs.*

Reproaches, Afflictions, Companions – the world looks at us like a rag-tag bunch of people with old time convictions – outdated and not hip, not open minded

Matt 7:13-14 Enter ye in at the strait gate: for wide *is* the gate, and broad *is* the way, that leadeth to destruction, and many there be which go in thereat: Because strait *is* the gate, and narrow *is* the way, which leadeth unto life, and few there be that find it.

Verse 34

Your companions will change when you get saved…a person who claims to be saved but wants to hang around with the old crowd of friends and keep company with the old bunch needs to examine himself.

2 Cor 13:5 Examine yourselves, whether ye be in the faith; prove your own selves. Know ye not your own selves, how that Jesus Christ is in you, except ye be reprobates?

(ill) Acts 9:1-8, 13-15, 19-20, 23-25

Your greatest friends after salvation will be the disciples of the Lord: Christians! They will pray for you, stand with you, be there for you…

Heb 11:24-25 By faith Moses, when he was come to years, refused to be called the son of Pharaoh's daughter; Choosing rather to suffer affliction with the people of God, than to enjoy the pleasures of sin for a season;

Verse 35

Cast not away – word picture of throwing out a cast net without any rope attached.

1 Cor 9:26-27 I therefore so run, not as uncertainly; so fight I, not as one that beateth the air: But I keep under my body, and bring *it* into subjection: lest that by any means, when I have preached to others, I myself should be a castaway.

Confidence – when you forget where you came from (32) and who your people are (33), you will begin to "cast away" your assurance (confidence)

Ps 118:8 *It is* better to trust in the LORD than to put confidence in man.

Ps 118:9 *It is* better to trust in the LORD than to put confidence in princes.

Prov 3:26 For the LORD shall be thy confidence, and shall keep thy foot from being taken.

Isa 30:15 For thus saith the Lord GOD, the Holy One of Israel; In returning and rest shall ye be saved; in quietness and in confidence shall be your strength: and ye would not.

2 Thes 3:4 And we have confidence in the Lord touching you, that ye both do and will do the things which we command you.

1 John 2:28 And now, little children, abide in him; that, when he shall appear, we may have confidence, and not be ashamed before him at his coming.

Great recompence of reward – when a child of God loses his confidence in the Lord they will begin questioning and doubting everything around them.

Doubt and confusion are not of the Lord

1 Cor 14:33 For God is not *the author* of confusion, but of peace, as in all churches of the saints.

Ps 71:1 In thee, O LORD, do I put my trust: let me never be put to confusion.

Confusion - "to become pale or anemic; to have no heart or hope"

Verse 36

Ye have need – greatest danger in a child of God's life – need nothing.

Rev 3:17 Because thou sayest, I am rich, and increased with goods, and have need of nothing; and knowest not that thou art wretched, and miserable, and poor, and blind, and naked:

Patience – "endurance, constancy, continuance with cheerfulness; (1828) The suffering of afflictions, pain, toil, calamity, provocation or other evil, with a calm, unruffled temper; endurance without murmuring or fretfulness; A calm temper which bears evils without murmuring or discontent."

Receive the promise – knowing the promises, believing the promises and receiving the promises are all different and separate things. You can know the promises but not believe in them and you can believe in them but not receive them. Why? No patience with God or man.

(ill) I get impatient with a microwave at times

Verse 37

A little while –

(ill) A person changing jobs; quit old job took a break; begin a new job – with each step, counting down the days

John 7:33 Then said Jesus unto them, Yet a little while am I with you, and *then* I go unto him that sent me.

John 16:16-22

Every day is one day closer to the coming of the Lord.

Verse38

That expression appears three times in Word of God.

The Just – Rom 1:17 The book of Romans answers the question, Who is justified by God?

Rom 3:23-24 For all have sinned, and come short of the glory of God; Being justified freely by his grace through the redemption that is in Christ Jesus:

Shall live – Gal 3:11 The book of Galatians answers the question, How do the justified live?

Gal 2:20 I am crucified with Christ: nevertheless I live; yet not I, but Christ liveth in me: and the life which I now live in the flesh I live by the faith of the Son of God, who loved me, and gave himself for me.

By faith – Heb 10:38 The book of Hebrews answers the question, What is it that keeps the justified living for Jesus? By Faith

Hab 2:4 Behold, his soul *which* is lifted up is not upright in him: but the just shall live by his faith.

Your personal walk with God is between you and God and your faith in Him is what makes the difference. The next chapter is the "Hall of Faith" or the faith chapter. Chapter 11 defines, describes, develops, and defends faith.

Verse 39

We are not of them – the difference

Draw back – "to shrink; to become reprobate"

Perdition – "damnation"

Php 1:6 Being confident of this very thing, that he which hath begun a good work in you will perform *it* until the day of Jesus Christ:

(ill) Things I quit – football, scouts, trumpet…but when I got saved, he started it and he will finish it. "That's it; it's over. I started it; I will finish it."

CHAPTER 11

Every day of our lives we live by faith. Common faith is that faith exercised in everyday life. No one can live a single day without faith. Faith in food we eat, banks we use, post offices we mail our mail at, doctors we visit, buildings we walk into. Some of the faith we exercise is unnoticed by us and then again some faith we make a determined choice to exercise it without realizing it is faith; i.e. making the choice to go to a doctor for some sickness. Spiritual faith is similar. Saving faith is placing a confidence in the Savior, Jesus Christ, to save from sin.

(ill) The Muslim puts his faith in the Koran and Muhammad; the idolater puts his faith in his graven image; the humanist puts his faith in himself; the philosopher puts his faith in his own ideas; the materialist puts his faith in his money; and the religious person puts his faith in his own good works. None of these can save, because of the object of faith, in each case, is wrong.

Acts 4:12 Neither is there salvation in any other: for there is none other name under heaven given among men, whereby we must be saved.

The Christian life begins with personal faith in the Lord Jesus Christ. The life of a child of God from the moment of salvation is a journey of faith living. We live by the faith of the Son of God, (Eph 2:20). Hebrews 12:2 states that Jesus Christ is the author and finisher of our faith. Chapter 11 is the chapter that will define, describe, defend and for the child of God actually DEVELOP faith in our lives. Rom 10:17 So then faith *cometh* by hearing, and hearing by the word of God.

For an outline of this chapter:

The Explanation of Faith – verse 1
The Elders of Faith – verse 2
The Education of Faith – verse 3

The Examples of Faith – verse 4-40 All of the heroes of faith saw their faith result in triumph over the 1) IMMEDIATE circumstances of life 2) IMPOSSIBLE circumstances of life 3) INCORPORATED circumstances of life i.e. The situations in our life that we try to live apart from the Son of God are the things that defeat us. An amazing thing about the word faith – 231 times in Word of God. Only two times in OT (Deut 32:20; Hab 2:4); the rest are found in NT (229 times). The first time in NT - Matt 6:30 Wherefore, if God so clothe the grass of the field, which to day is, and to morrow is cast into the oven, *shall he* not much more *clothe* you, O ye of little faith?

Basically there are three types of faith recorded – 1) Little 2) Great, {Luke 7:1-10} 3) No, {Mark 4:40} – but no matter what condition your faith is in, it needs to increase and grow! No matter what condition your faith is in, there is hope.

Luke 17:5-6; Mark 4:30-32

"Bible faith is confident obedience to God's Word in spite of circumstances and consequences."

Verse 1

Now – faith is a DAILY active foundational ingredient to the child of God's life. 2 Peter 1:5-6; Heb 10:38

Substance – "concrete foundation; (1828) the essential part; something real, not imaginary; something solid, not empty."

Evidence – "conviction; (1828) proof; to make clear to the mind" Faith gives the child of God an advantage over the carnal mind in that we understand God truths by faith.

Faith is almost a "sixth sense" that only saved people possess. The eye takes hold on the light waves, the ear takes hold of the sound waves, the nose takes hold of odors, our touch takes hold of feeling, our tongue takes hold of taste – but faith takes hold of God. It connects us to God with a greater sense than our natural five senses.

Rom 8:7 Because the carnal mind *is* enmity against God: for it is not subject to the law of God, neither indeed can be.

Verse 2

Good report – "record; testimony" God is keeping record of everything that we do by faith. That is what chapter 11 is; God's record of people who lived by faith. **Two thoughts** – 1) God's book contains only what we have done by faith. Glory to God! 2) God's book contains only what we have done by faith. Oh my! What is in my book? How much is in my book?

Mal 3:16-17 Then they that feared the LORD spake often one to another: and the LORD hearkened, and heard *it*, and a book of remembrance was written before him for them that feared the LORD, and that thought upon his name. And they shall be mine, saith the LORD of hosts, in that day when I make up my jewels; and I will spare them, as a man spareth his own son that serveth him.

Verse 3

Understand – Faith will EXPAND your wisdom. Scientists are so limited because they believe only what evidence they can see. We believe God's Word and see further and greater than any scientist or Hubble telescope.

(ill) Google, "How did the universe begin?" **Best Answer**: "The universe began with the 'big bang.' The universe started to expand and cool rapidly. Some time passed and sub atomic particles where [*sic*] created along with mass that clumped together to form stars, planets and galaxies. The stars via their nuclear furnace created newer and heavier elements." **Another Answer**: "There are lots of theories about our beginning, God not being a legitimate one. Some say the Big Bang was caused by our universe colliding with another one (possibly of a higher dimension) or when it was split from another. Think of our universe as a bubble floating in the 'Void' (space between universes and dimensions) floating among other Universes. When a bubble collides with another, a new universe is created. When a bubble splits, two new universes are created. According

105

to String Theory, there are an infinite number of parallel universes, each one created when there is a new possibility. I know this may be difficult to comprehend but all of this is theoretical. No hard evidence has been discovered of any of these theories. Another theory is that our Universe is nothing but a computer simulation of a futuristic Civilization, which is not that likely but Y'never know. Hope this helps."

There is no room for God and a Designer/Creator in the mind of an evolutionist. All is the end product of the random working of the blind forces of chance over billions of years. When it comes to the origin of our existence, science is confessedly theoretical.

Gen 1 – "And God said" the Word of God creating -

The Trinity in Creation – John 1:1; Col 1:15-17; Heb 1:1-3; 2 Pet 3:

Everything that God created has His seal of the Trinity upon it.

Light – (his first words in the Bible – let there be light) The light that we see (white light) is made up of what scientists call the "Primary colors of light" which are three colors red, green and blue.

Conception of new life – Man, woman, child

Human – Body, soul, spirit (1 Thes 5:23)

Solar System – There are three astronomical bodies: star, planet, moon

Fire – needs three things to ignite and exist: heat, fuel, oxygen

Water – made up of three parts: H_2O – two parts hydrogen and one part oxygen

Atoms – consist of three parts: proton, electron, neutron

Time – past, present, future

Earth – land, sea, air

Sun – three rays; beta, gamma, UV

Heaven – 1st, 2nd, 3rd

Habitation of the Damned – hell, bottomless pit, lake of fire

Verse 4

Abel – Faith Witnessing – Gen 4

It is no accident that the first account of faith being exercised by an individual is Abel. Abel was murdered for his faith. The faith of Abel produced jealousy, envy, hatred and an act of murder in the heart of his own brother, Cain. Your faith affects others. It rattles their faith.

(ill) Atheist shaken because a Christian prays. They want to boycott and outlaw our praying to a God that they say does not exist.

(ill) Agnostic – A man and I visiting another man in the hospital. His brother was in the room and my visiting partner asked him if he went to church anywhere. "No, I'm going to be perfectly honest with you; I'm an agnostic."

Offered – Why did these boys offer? (ill) His parents surely told them about the garden and what God did to cover their sin and shame; Gen 3, Cain offered the fruit of the ground, Abel offered the firstling of the flock. Why? Every man has a God consciousness about him. Body – self-consciousness; soul – world consciousness; spirit – God consciousness.

Ps 19:1-3 The heavens declare the glory of God; and the firmament sheweth his handywork. Day unto day uttereth speech, and night unto night sheweth knowledge. *There is* no speech nor language, *where* their voice is not heard.

Rom 1:20 For the invisible things of him from the creation of the world are clearly seen, being understood by the things that are made, *even* his eternal power and Godhead; so that they are without excuse:

They know that there is a true and living God – the only way to deny Him is through education – 1 Cor 1:21 For after that in the wisdom of God the world by wisdom knew not God, it pleased God by the foolishness of preaching to save them that believe.

(ill) Native Indian sitting in front of a totem pole with gods carved into it, worshipping the god of his imagination. Why? A God consciousness. His spirit is dead in trespasses and sins, therefore he can only imagine what God must be like. But when

107

the true and living God presents Himself to that man, God gives him the spiritual faith needed to trust in His Son and then a choice must be made.

What did these boys offer? One offered his own works, the other offered the best, he offered blood and he also offered a body. An innocent (lamb) sacrificed its life in order to cover the sin and shame of Adam and Eve.

Verse 5

Enoch – Faith Walking – Gen 5:21-24

Interesting to note what Enoch's name means - "dedicated; disciplined"

Period of time that Enoch lived – right before the flood.

Pleased God – how? By walking by faith

Only two men in the Bible who walked with God – Enoch and Noah

Gen 6:9 These *are* the generations of Noah: Noah was a just man *and* perfect in his generations, *and* Noah walked with God.

Enoch - only man in the Bible who never will die – picture of those alive and remaining at the coming of the Lord – 1 Thes 4:1-12

Enoch prophesied of the Lord's coming – Jude 14,15

The Book of the Generation – (only 2x) Gen 5; Matt 1 – book of Adam or book of Jesus – 1 Cor 15:22

Verse 6

Impossible –

Two Musts – 1) Reality of God 2) Rewards of God

Diligently – "search out; seek with all your heart"

Isa 55:6-7 Seek ye the LORD while he may be found, call ye upon him while he is near: Let the wicked forsake his way, and the unrighteous man his thoughts: and let him return unto the LORD, and he will have mercy upon him; and to our God, for he will abundantly pardon.

Jer 29:11-13 For I know the thoughts that I think toward you, saith the LORD, thoughts of peace, and not of evil, to give you an expected end. Then shall ye call upon me, and ye shall go and pray unto me, and I will hearken unto you. And ye shall seek me, and find *me*, when ye shall search for me with all your heart.

Promise of Revival? – 2Chron 7:14 If my people, which are called by my name, shall humble themselves, and pray, and seek my face, and turn from their wicked ways; then will I hear from heaven, and will forgive their sin, and will heal their land. (Seeking His face, not His hand or hand outs)

(ill) Text I received – "Bro Dell, I had the privilege of praying for you and yours this morning. I read somewhere that LOVERS LOVE TO BE ALONE TOGETHER. If this statement is true and I claim to love the Lord with all my heart, soul, and mind, then I would feel compelled to spend much time in secret with HIM. May we feel compelled to spend much time with HIM especially during a season so occupied with other interests. We desperately need HIM now. Stay faithful."

Verse 7

Noah – Faith Working – Gen 6:11-13; 17 – 6:22; 7:5

Warned - "to give notice of approaching or probable danger or evil, that it might be avoided; to inform previously; to give notice to"

Noah was warned by God over 100 years before the flood took place. There were no signs that such a catastrophic thing would happen other than evil men waxing worse and worse. For a full century things continued as they were – getting worse as men carried out their daily lives.

Jer 6:10 To whom shall I speak, and give warning, that they may hear? behold, their ear *is* uncircumcised, and they cannot hearken: behold, the word of the LORD is unto them a reproach; they have no delight in it.

Ezekiel 3:17-21; Ezekiel 33:1-7

Acts 20:31 Therefore watch, and remember, that by the space of three years I ceased not to warn every one night and day with tears.

Things not seen as yet – It had never rained upon the earth and certainly not a flood of waters

Fear - Ps 36:1 The transgression of the wicked saith within my heart, *that there is* no fear of God before his eyes.

1) A man is not wise until he fears God Almighty Ps 111:10 The fear of the LORD *is* the beginning of wisdom: a good understanding have all they that do *his commandments*: his praise endureth for ever.

2) If a man truly fears God he will live right - Ps 119:63 I *am* a companion of all *them* that fear thee, and of them that keep thy precepts. Ps 128:1 A Song of degrees. Blessed *is* every one that feareth the LORD; that walketh in his ways.

3) Fearing God is a conscious choice that a man makes - Prov 1:29 For that they hated knowledge, and did not choose the fear of the LORD:

4) When a man chooses not to fear God, he will fear everything else and destroy himself - Rom 3:16-18 Destruction and misery *are* in their ways: And the way of peace have they not known: There is no fear of God before their eyes.

Fearing God will:

1) Produce hatred for sin - Prov 8:13 The fear of the LORD *is* to hate evil: pride, and arrogancy, and the evil way, and the froward mouth, do I hate.

2) Causes you to live longer - Prov 10:27 The fear of the LORD prolongeth days: but the years of the wicked shall be shortened.

3) Builds Confidence - Prov 14:26 In the fear of the LORD *is* strong confidence: and his children shall have a place of refuge.

4) Satisfies your life - Prov 19:23 The fear of the LORD *tendeth* to life: and *he that hath it* shall abide satisfied; he shall not be visited with evil.

5) Pleases God - Ps 147:11 The LORD taketh pleasure in them that fear him, in those that hope in his mercy.

6) Prospered the early church - Acts 9:31 Then had the churches rest throughout all Judaea and Galilee and Samaria, and were edified; and walking in the fear of the Lord, and in the comfort of the Holy Ghost, were multiplied.

It is said about the days of Noah – Luke 17:26-27 – 2 Pet 2:5-6

Condemned the world – "I told you so"

Verse 8

Abraham – Faith Willing

Abraham lived in the pagan regions of Ur of the Chaldees. They were moon worshippers, and Abraham probably was also. He was a Gentile man about to be separated by God unto a new life and become the father of the faithful.

The account of Abraham's life is covered in more verses than any other hero of faith in Hebrews 11. Twelve verses detail what God considered the "by faith" moments of Abraham's life. The actual account of Abraham's life as covered in this chapter begins in Gen 11 and continues through Gen 22 – Twelve chapters.

Obeyed – His willing obedience involved two things:

1) His SENSITIVITY to God's voice – the most important thing in anyone's life – hearing the voice of God.

How does someone develop a sensitivity to the voice of God? A realization that God speaks (ill) First time the voice of God is mentioned in Bible – Gen 3:8-10 And they heard the voice of the LORD God walking in the garden in the cool of the day: and Adam and his wife hid themselves from the presence of the LORD God amongst the trees of the garden. And the LORD God called unto Adam, and said unto him, Where *art* thou? And he said, I heard thy voice in the garden, and I was afraid, because I *was* naked; and I hid myself.

– Adam was hiding from the voice of God because of sin. The child of God has been forgiven of all sin and the voice of God is recorded for us to listen to. John 10:3-4 To him the porter openeth; and the sheep hear his voice: and he calleth his own sheep by name, and leadeth them out. And when he putteth forth his own sheep, he goeth before them, and the sheep follow him: for they know his voice. Ex 23:22 But if thou shalt indeed obey his voice, and do all that I speak; then I will be an enemy unto thine enemies, and an adversary unto thine adversaries.

(ill) Hold your Bible in front of you and say, "Speak, Lord, for thy servant heareth."

2) His SEPARATION from his old life – (LOT)

We are to put off the old man and put on the new man.

Abraham's future depended on his obedience to the voice of God; but his family's future depended on his obedience – yea, our lives depended on Abraham's obedience.

He began a journey but in the wrong direction and wound up in the wrong location. Every time we let the old man lead – DISOBEDIENCE will be dealt with, DELAY of the blessings of God, and then we have to experience and wait on the DEATH of the old man.

"God is not able to work through us because He spends so much time working on us!"

Your past will:

1) Hinder your journey
2) Haunt your mind
3) Hurt your loved ones

Php 3:13-15 Brethren, I count not myself to have apprehended: but *this* one thing *I do*, forgetting those things which are behind, and reaching forth unto those things which are before, I press toward the mark for the prize of the high calling of God in Christ Jesus. Let us therefore, as many as be perfect, be thus minded: and if in any thing ye be otherwise minded, God shall reveal even this unto you.

Not knowing – a picture of the life of a Christian. God shows us one day at a time. He may show us a dream of our future, but the exact data of us reaching that dream is day by day. (ill) Paul's journey of faith – Phil 3:12-16

What if God would show you your future in advance? God teaches us to live by faith by leading us one day at a time. His mercies are new every morning. His guidance is faithful.

Verse 9

Sojourned – "to live in a place as a temporary resident; to live as a stranger for a time." When Abraham entered the land of promise, he found it to be already inhabited by heathen. He did not apply their way of living to himself but considered himself a stranger in a strange land. The inhabitants looked at Abraham as strange, but he also looked at them as strange.

With Isaac and Jacob – the faith that Abraham lived by was passed down to his sons.

Same promise – what God promised me, He will do for you! We live by the faith of the Lord Jesus Christ (Gal 2:20). The covenant we enter into when we get saved is a covenant that was made among the Trinity. God is setting that covenant in place through Abram. Galatians 3:6-9, 13-16

Verse 10

Faith encompasses our entire life –
Verse 8 Abraham LISTENED by faith
Verse 9 Abraham LIVED by faith
Verse 10 Abraham LOOKED by faith
We have got to keep in mind that these OT characters were real people. They were like us. They had heartaches, sorrows, and other difficulties. At times, they soared like the eagle in their faith, trusting God with complete obedience. Other times, they plunged to the depths of frailty and faltering faith, but they pursued by faith. We may utterly fail today, but tomorrow lends to us a new day of mercy to go on and look for the promise that only God can build in our lives.

Abraham looked for what God could provide, not what his surrounding world could offer. He truly lived out verse 6 of

Hebrews 11. He believed that God was and was able to reward him.

Verse 11

Sara received strength – Gen 18:9-15; Gen 21:1-6

Judged – "to consider; to think about; to esteem" A promise is only as good as the character of the one making the promise. "I promise" can only be fulfilled by one who is able and willing to be a person of their word.

Verse 12

As good as dead – Abraham's original name was Abram. His name means, "a father of many." When Abram would meet someone and they asked his name, the next question would be, "Well, how many children do you have?" None would be his reply. You can't even live up to your name. Later in the life of Abram, God shows up and confronts his inability with God's supernatural ability. Gen 17:1-7 Abram – 2 syllable; Abraham – 3 syllable. God is now involved in the life of Abraham. Now, with Abraham (father of a multitude) and God his life would be abundantly fruitful.

Dust of the earth (Gen 13:15-16) – physical seed through Isaac, who pictured the death of Jesus Christ

Stars of the sky (Gen 15:1-5) – spiritual seed through Jesus Christ, who actually died

Romans 4:1-5, 16-25 "Father Abraham"

Verse 13

Having not received ("promise(s)") - Abraham lived his life sojourning never living in the land of promise. He received the promise of Isaac being born.

John Phillips – "The land was as safe and as sure as though they had already conquered and colonized it, because God had promised it. God's promissory notes are drawn by His own hand

and cannot fail. A promise from God is a more sure thing than a post-dated check from a billionaire."

(ill) We are more than conquerors through him that loved us. If God be for us who can be against us? When we enter a battle, rest assured we are going to come through it victorious. Look at Romans 8 – "I see you, you persuaded me, I embrace you, and I confess I will come forth a victor!"

They – 1) Saw them 2) Were Persuaded ("to be confident; to make friends") 3) Embraced them ("to embrace so tightly, you become one") 4) Confessed – "I'm just a passing through; my treasures are laid up somewhere beyond the blue".

Verse 14

Declare plainly – "to disclose by words" I'm seeking a better place than this!

(ill) Christmas at mama's. A man came by (apples, cabbage out of his garden). "John, you look so good. You ok? You've been sick haven't you? How's your health?" Heaven holds a healing for me! Amen. He pulled me off to the side, "I want you to know that all that work you put into me paid off. I'm telling my kids about Jesus now."

Seek – No COMPROMISE

Verse 15

Mindful – No CONTEMPLATION – they burned the bridges back to the old life.

Verse 16

Desire – No COMPARISON

1 Cor 2:9-10 But as it is written, Eye hath not seen, nor ear heard, neither have entered into the heart of man, the things which God hath prepared for them that love him. But God hath revealed *them* unto us by his Spirit: for the Spirit searcheth all things, yea, the deep things of God. 2 Cor 4:17-18 For our light affliction,

which is but for a moment, worketh for us a far more exceeding *and* eternal weight of glory; While we look not at the things which are seen, but at the things which are not seen: for the things which are seen *are* temporal; but the things which are not seen *are* eternal. Rom 8:18 For I reckon that the sufferings of this present time *are* not worthy *to be compared* with the glory which shall be revealed in us.

Not ashamed to be called – All through the OT, I am the God of Abraham, Isaac, and Jacob – This same God is MY God!

Isa 41:10 Fear thou not; for I *am* with thee: be not dismayed; for I *am* thy God: I will strengthen thee; yea, I will help thee; yea, I will uphold thee with the right hand of my righteousness.

Verse 17

Tried – Gen 22:1 Tempt – "to prove; to try" a temptation is a trial; it is a test. Something in our lives is being put to the test; placed on trial.

Jas 1:12 Blessed *is* the man that endureth temptation: for when he is tried, he shall receive the crown of life, which the Lord hath promised to them that love him.

God is going to TRY your faith. James 1:2-3 "Glory to God, I'm going through another trial." Not for God to see what you can do; but so you might see what God will do! 1 Peter 4:12-13 – God is going to take some sin out of your life. 1 Peter 4:1-2

God is going to PROVE your love. God is going to CLEANSE your life.

Verse 19

Accounting – "to take an inventory; to estimate; to conclude; calculating"

The arithmetic of God. Even when God subtracts, He is adding; and He will subtract the temporal to add the eternal!

God had promised that He was going to give a son to Abraham in his old age; that son also would be the promised seed that

116

would reproduce and become as the sand of the seashore and the stars of heaven.

Gen 15:3-6 Abraham believed the Lord's promise about this boy before he was born and even more so after Isaac was born.

In a figure – in Abraham's mind, even if God took the boy's life, He was well able to raise him from the dead. He knew and believed that God was going to use his son. **In Abraham's TEMPTATION, his TRUST prevailed and triumphed.** {Isaac has no children at the time of Genesis 22. Abraham remembered the miracle of the PAST in his son.}

Galatians 3:6-9

Verse 20

Every person listed in Hebrews 11 had one thing in common – faith! They lived by faith, accomplished things by faith, and died by faith. Faith is the common element of all our lives that covers our past, our present and our future.

1 Peter 1:7-9 – the end of your faith. Faith will come to an end: for some at death, for others at the coming of the Lord. Jesus Christ is the author and finisher of our faith.

Php 1:6 Being confident of this very thing, that he which hath begun a good work in you will perform *it* until the day of Jesus Christ:

Faith has a beginning and an end in our lives…Gal 3:23 But before faith came, we were kept under the law, shut up unto the faith which should afterwards be revealed. Gal 3:25 But after that faith is come, we are no longer under a schoolmaster. Gal 3:26 For ye are all the children of God by faith in Christ Jesus.

The only way for us to have a happy future is to have faith in the Lord Jesus Christ. (ill) A dad took his son to the pet shop to pick out a puppy. After looking at all the dogs, there was one wagging his tail. His son said, "Dad, I want the one with the happy end."

Jer 29:11 For I know the thoughts that I think toward you, saith the LORD, thoughts of peace, and not of evil, to give you an expected end.

117

It has been said of Isaac, "He was an ordinary son of a great father and an ordinary father of a great son." Not much is said about Isaac in the Scriptures.

One truth about Isaac is found in the word "love." Gen 22 is the first mention of love; the love of a father toward his son. The second time the word love is found in Scripture is found in Gen 24:67; that loved son loving his wife!

He loved his wife and intreated the Lord for his wife Rebekah because she was barren. He took her at the age of 40, prayed for her 20 years and at the age of 60, she bears him twins – Esau and Jacob. The main thing about Isaac's life – he loved his family and redug the wells that his father Abraham had dug, Gen 26.

Isaac, by faith blessed Jacob and Esau on his death bed. His eyes were now dim; he could not see by sight so he saw by faith. Esau was the firstborn and the rightful heir to the fortune of Isaac. Isaac loved Esau, but Rebekah loved Jacob. As the firstborn, Esau had rights to: 1) the noted position that the Messiah would be born through 2) the family head or family priest 3) a double portion of the material property. The material possessions were the only thing that Esau was interested in.

God had prophesied about the two boys – Gen 25:23 because He knew what they would do in their self-will. (Foreknowledge of God)

The family blessing did go to Jacob who later became Israel. Esau got a blessing but it was a secondary blessing with no rights to anything spiritual.

Mal 1:2-3 I have loved you, saith the LORD. Yet ye say, Wherein hast thou loved us? *Was* not Esau Jacob's brother? saith the LORD: yet I loved Jacob, And I hated Esau, and laid his mountains and his heritage waste for the dragons of the wilderness.

Verse 21

Jacob became Israel (Gen 32). Now the blessing goes from an individual to a tribe. The two sons of Joseph (Jacob's favorite son) were born while Joseph was in Egypt. Joseph had found favor with God and had been exalted to the second position in Egypt. He had taken a Gentile bride and Ephraim and Manasseh had been born through them. Jacob had the two boys in front of him and crisscrossed his hands knowingly giving the right hand blessing unto Ephraim, the younger son. Jacob did this in prophetic worship knowing that the elder would serve the younger. Ephraim became so mighty that even after the 12 tribes split, the 10 tribes that made up the northern kingdom was often called Ephraim.

Verse 22

It is important to live right but it is even more important to die right. In the account of Joseph, you would think that the Hebrews account would talk about the faith Joseph had while he lived; but it gives his dying faith account. Joseph's life is one of the most beautiful and rich accounts in all the word of God that typifies the life of Christ. He was betrayed by his brethren and lived his life in a strange land. He was lied about, mistreated, abused, and forgotten. Yet, the Bible keeps saying, "And God was with Joseph." The things Joseph experienced in life could have made him bitter, but they only made him better - more like Christ.

Made mention – Joseph died believing the promise that the children of Israel would be led out of the land of Egypt back into the promised land.

His bones – "I'm not of this world." As an incentive to the nation of Israel, carry my bones back to the promised land with you. (Gen 50:22-26). Moses left with his bones (Ex 13:19) but never made it into the promised land. The nation of Israel fulfilled Joseph's wish in Joshua 24:32.

"Not a bone" of Joseph was left in Egypt (type of the world). Eph 5:29-30 For no man ever yet hated his own flesh; but nourisheth and cherisheth it, even as the Lord the church: For we are members of his body, of his flesh, and of his bones.

The Lord's bones (us) are just embalmed right now, one day as His dead body rose from the grave – the body of the Lord is going to come forth and not a bone of His will be left behind.

Verse 23
Moses – "The Five Faiths of Moses" Verse 23-29
1) Only a Child
Their faith was courageous. To oppose the decree of Pharaoh meant certain death.

Verse 24-26
2) Old enough to make a Choice
2 Tim 1:5 When I call to remembrance the unfeigned faith that is in thee, which dwelt first in thy grandmother Lois, and thy mother Eunice; and I am persuaded that in thee also.
He refused the 1) social position 2) sinful pleasures 3) suggested prosperity

Verse 27
3) Oppression and Opposition were Corrupting

Verse 28
4) Ordinances were Commanded

Verse 29
5) Others were Counting on him
Assaying – the world cannot do what the child of God can do by faith.
Money, education, power, prestige, popularity will never replace or come close to faith. Faith is trusting God when the circumstances and the world say it can't be done. Money and education do not impress God – but faith in God does.

Verse 30

When you study online the subject of Jericho, you will find that there are conflicting finds in the field of archaeological science. In the 1950's a British team excavated the site and their conclusion was – "there was no archaeological data to prove that a wall existed around Jericho." In the 1990's another team found evidence that a wall did exist. No matter the findings – the Bible is accurate and without error.

Joshua 6 is the Biblical account. Seven priests bearing seven trumpets of ram's horns led the company, followed by priests carrying the ark of the covenant. Behind them followed men of war. Every day for six days they would walk around the entire city. On the 7th day, they went around seven times and after the last time, the priests blew with their trumpets and the people of God shouted with a shout then the walls fell down flat.

Jericho stood in the way of the people of God advancing and entering into the promised land. The nation of Israel, to the people of Jericho must have looked foolish. Faith is not unreasonable nor is it foolish. It may look unreasonable but faith undermines human wisdom.

1 Corinthians talks a lot about foolishness.

1 Cor 1:18 For the preaching of the cross is to them that perish foolishness; but unto us which are saved it is the power of God.

1 Cor 1:21 For after that in the wisdom of God the world by wisdom knew not God, it pleased God by the foolishness of preaching to save them that believe.

1 Cor 1:23-25 But we preach Christ crucified, unto the Jews a stumblingblock, and unto the Greeks foolishness; But unto them which are called, both Jews and Greeks, Christ the power of God, and the wisdom of God. Because the foolishness of God is wiser than men; and the weakness of God is stronger than men.

The natural man bases his conclusions on that which seems **rational** to him. The believer rests his convictions on that which has been **revealed** to him.

Joshua 6:26 – anyone rebuilding Jericho would be cursed with the death of his children; fulfilled in 1 Kings 16:34 In his days did Hiel the Bethelite build Jericho: he laid the foundation thereof in Abiram his firstborn, and set up the gates thereof in his youngest *son* Segub, according to the word of the LORD, which he spake by Joshua the son of Nun.

Verse 31

Jericho was a doomed city. Even with all of its fortresses and walls, Jericho was history. Gentile receiving Jewish spies. Not just a gentile but a sinful harlot. What motivated this sinful woman to act in faith? What she had heard, she believed.

Josh 2:9-11 – let them down by a scarlet cord to safety. That same scarlet thread that brought us to safety, shall be safety for you. Josh 2:18-19

Rahab is in the genealogy of Jesus Christ – Matt 1:5

1) The Declaration of her faith – we have heard
2) The Demonstration of her faith – scarlet line
3) The Deliverance of her faith – perished not

Verse 32

4 judges; 1 king; 1 prophet by name and the whole host of prophets unnamed.

4 judges lived during a time when there was no king in Israel; every man was doing that which was right in his own eyes. Whenever someone is doing that which is right in his own eyes, he is doing what is wrong in the eyes of God.

Prov 14:12 There is a way which seemeth right unto a man, but the end thereof *are* the ways of death.

Notice: not one sin of these men is mentioned, only what they did by faith.

For example, the most noted of the judges mentioned – Samson; known for his supernatural strength became like any other man because he played games with the power of God in his life at the lap of Delilah. But the book of Hebrews mentions none of that; it simply mentions his faith.

David – the time of triumph; Israel had a king after God's own heart. But he had to escape the edge of the sword 24 different times when Saul tried to personally kill him or arranged for him to be killed. He refused to retaliate even when it looked like God had given his enemy into his hand. Without a NT to study, and the example of Christ before him, David behaved himself in the likeness of Christ.

1 Pet 2:21-23 For even hereunto were ye called: because Christ also suffered for us, leaving us an example, that ye should follow his steps: Who did no sin, neither was guile found in his mouth: Who, when he was reviled, reviled not again; when he suffered, he threatened not; but committed *himself* to him that judgeth righteously:

Verse 33

Subdued kingdoms – Moses and Aaron stood in faithfulness to God's Word

Wrought righteousness – Joseph

Obtained promises - Ruth

Stopped the mouths of lions – Daniel

Verse 34

Violence of fire – Meshach, Shadrach, Abednego thrown into the fiery furnace

Escaped the sword – 100 prophets hid in a cave by Obadiah when Jezebel was on a rampage (1 Kings 18)

Weakness into strength – Elijah outnumbered by 850:1

Valiant in fight – Joshua, a valiant man leading into the promised land

Verse 35

Dead raised – Woman of Shunem miraculously given a son who died when he was grown. She would not quit until Elisha came; her son revived. (2 Kings 4)

And others, tortured – rather than renounce their faith, they gladly received the torture

Verse 36

And others - Some recorded in OT, some not – but God was watching and keeping record

Imprisonment – Jeremiah

Verse 37

Sawn asunder – Tradition is that the evil King Manasseh had the prophet Isaiah placed in the hollow trunk of a tree and then commanded the tree to be sawn in two.

Verse 38

Counted as the filth and scourge of the earth, but God says, "Of whom the world was not worthy." They weren't promise keepers; they were Living by Faith.

When reading this list, you can't help but see glimpses of Jesus Christ in the lives of these people.

Isa 52:13-14 Behold, my servant shall deal prudently, he shall be exalted and extolled, and be very high. As many were astonied at thee; his visage was so marred more than any man, and his form more than the sons of men:

Isa 53:3-5 He is despised and rejected of men; a man of sorrows, and acquainted with grief: and we hid as it were *our* faces from him; he was despised, and we esteemed him not. Surely he hath borne our griefs, and carried our sorrows: yet we did esteem him stricken, smitten of God, and afflicted. But he *was* wounded for our transgressions, *he was* bruised for our iniquities: the chastisement of our peace *was* upon him; and with his stripes we are healed. Isa 53:7-11 He was oppressed, and he was afflicted, yet he opened not his mouth: he is brought as a lamb to the slaughter, and as a sheep before her shearers is dumb, so he openeth not his mouth. He was taken from prison and from judgment: and who shall declare his generation? for he was cut off out of the land of the living: for the transgression of my people was he stricken. And he made his grave with the wicked, and with the rich in his death; because he had done no violence, neither *was any* deceit in his mouth. Yet it pleased the LORD to bruise him; he hath put *him* to grief: when thou shalt make his soul an offering for sin, he shall see *his* seed, he shall prolong *his* days, and the pleasure of the LORD shall prosper in his hand. He shall see of the travail of his soul, *and* shall be satisfied:

Verse 39

There they stand, the ones who were looking forward to the coming of the Messiah. All the promises were in front of them. No NT, no indwelling of the Holy Spirit to teach and guide, living under the law – GOOD REPORT!

Verse 40

This great cloud of witnesses is waiting on us. They had the shadow; we have the substance. They had good things; we have the better. They had the typology; we have the Testator of the NT. He is setting up His next chapter by putting His readers in remembrance of what has already been done by faith.

CHAPTER 12

Verse 1

Wherefore – whenever we see a wherefore, we must ask ourselves what it is there for. Wherefore - "for what reason; for what cause"

The writer has given us example after example of those who have finished their course by faith and crossed the finish line. – wherefore

The Christian life is described in many facets –

1) Soldier

2 Tim 2:3 Thou therefore endure hardness, as a good soldier of Jesus Christ.

2) Ambassador

2 Cor 5:20 Now then we are ambassadors for Christ, as though God did beseech *you* by us: we pray *you* in Christ's stead, be ye reconciled to God.

3) Part of a family

Eph 2:19 Now therefore ye are no more strangers and foreigners, but fellowcitizens with the saints, and of the household of God;

4) Sheep

John 10:27 My sheep hear my voice, and I know them, and they follow me:

5) Fishers of men

Mark 1:17 And Jesus said unto them, Come ye after me, and I will make you to become fishers of men.

Now, he surrounds our life with the grandstand of OT heroes and encourages us to run our race.

1 Cor 9:24-26; Phil 3:13-14

Acts 20:24 But none of these things move me, neither count I my life dear unto myself, so that I might finish my course with joy, and the ministry, which I have received of the Lord Jesus, to testify the gospel of the grace of God.

Let us – Put off

(ill) Man went to his doctor and told him, "I have back trouble." The doctor examined him and said, "No you don't have back trouble, you have front trouble. You lose some weight and your back will quit hurting. Lose the excess weight up front, and it will help your back feel better."

(ill) During practice sessions, runners will run with extra weight so that when the real race comes, they will feel lighter and be more apt to run a better time during the race. This is not practice; this is the real race.

Weight – not necessarily sin, but it hinders us from becoming all that we could be without it. Watching too much TV, spending more time on FB than with your face in the Book, anything that attracts your attention to where it distracts you from the things of God.

Sin – whatever is not right

1 John 5:17 All unrighteousness is sin:

Besets - "to surround; to hem in; to encompass; to set a fence around" It has become a stronghold in your life and you are not doing the sin, the sin is doing you.

Patience – this is not a 100-yard dash; this is a marathon that begins the day you get saved and will end the day you go to heaven.

Rom 5:3 And not only *so*, but we glory in tribulations also: knowing that tribulation worketh patience;

Jas 1:3 Knowing *this*, that the trying of your faith worketh patience.

Many children of God begin with a dash, but then when trouble or trials come, they quit running and place themselves on the bench.

Gal 5:7 Ye did run well; who did hinder you that ye should not obey the truth?

Verse 2

Verse 1, the writer surrounds us with the cloud of witnesses; now in verse 2 he sets our focus on our Coach at the finish line. You cannot run this race while looking around you at the cloud of witnesses, nor the other runners. You must keep your eyes set toward the finish line where your Head Coach is waiting to congratulate you with the words, "Well done thou good and faithful servant." Looking – to concentrate on;

Author and finisher – Author - "one who produces, creates or brings into being anything especially a book"

Php 1:6 Being confident of this very thing, that he which hath begun a good work in you will perform *it* until the day of Jesus Christ:

Mal 3:16 Then they that feared the LORD spake often one to another: and the LORD hearkened, and heard *it*, and a book of remembrance was written before him for them that feared the LORD, and that thought upon his name.

Jesus started this thing and he will finish it. (Gal 2:20)

Cross – the writer now points us to the cross; the implement of death. Cross now, crown later.

Mark 10:21 Then Jesus beholding him loved him, and said unto him, One thing thou lackest: go thy way, sell whatsoever thou hast, and give to the poor, and thou shalt have treasure in heaven: and come, take up the cross, and follow me.

1 Cor 1:18 For the preaching of the cross is to them that perish foolishness; but unto us which are saved it is the power of God.

Gal 6:14 But God forbid that I should glory, save in the cross of our Lord Jesus Christ, by whom the world is crucified unto me, and I unto the world.

Gal 6:17 From henceforth let no man trouble me: for I bear in my body the marks of the Lord Jesus.

Joy - Neh 8:10…neither be ye sorry; for the joy of the LORD is your strength.

Book of Philippians is the book of joy written by Paul while he was in prison to help us maintain our joy.

Joy, Endure, Despising – 3 words we must incorporate in our lives to finish right. If you love flowers, you will hate weeds. If you are going to finish well, you will have to keep the joy of the

Lord before you, endure your cross and despise those things that seem to hinder your race. To reach the throne of God right, you must do these things.

Looking – Look at:

His Person (Jesus)

His Power (author and finisher)

His Passion (joy)

His Pain (shame)

His Position (set down)

His Perspective (at the right hand of the throne of God) AS YOU LOOK AT HIM, HE IS WATCHING YOU!

Verse 3

Consider him – "evaluate; estimate; contemplate"

Contradiction against himself – the next time you are criticized; think on Jesus. The next time someone reproaches you; think on Him. The next time someone lies on you; think on Jesus. The next time someone laughs at you; think about Jesus. If anyone had the right to quit – Jesus had every reason and opportunity to quit.

Minds – the battle ground. Php 4:6-9 Be careful for nothing; but in every thing by prayer and supplication with thanksgiving let your requests be made known unto God. And the peace of God, which passeth all understanding, shall keep your hearts and minds through Christ Jesus. Finally, brethren, whatsoever things are true, whatsoever things *are* honest, whatsoever things *are* just, whatsoever things *are* pure, whatsoever things *are* lovely, whatsoever things *are* of good report; if *there be* any virtue, and if *there be* any praise, think on these things. Those things, which ye have both learned, and received, and heard, and seen in me, do: and the God of peace shall be with you.

Wearied and Faint – the mind becomes so encumbered with situations, things, thoughts…it becomes so tired and loaded down it wants to faint (relax, become weak, depressed, discouraged, not wanting to operate any longer).

Verse 4

Not yet resisted – the writer references us to the garden of Gethsemane. Jesus prayed so intensely that his sweat became as it were great drops of blood (Luke 22:44). He prayed earnestly.
Jas 5:16 Confess *your* faults one to another, and pray one for another, that ye may be healed. The effectual fervent prayer of a righteous man availeth much.

Verse 5

In context of putting away the sin that besets us and the fact that we have not striven against sin in prayer…chastisement.
Exhortation - "comfort; encouragement" We tend to think of chastisement in a false light as being "for others and never for me." We face certain things, physically, emotionally, financially, in the home – and we forget to consider that God may have us in the wood shed.
Isa 53:4 Surely he hath borne our griefs, and carried our sorrows: yet we did esteem him stricken, smitten of God, and afflicted.

Verse 6

Why is this happening to me? Because the Lord loves you. God is love! The hardest text to explain and preach.
Job 5:17-18 Behold, happy *is* the man whom God correcteth: therefore despise not thou the chastening of the Almighty: For he maketh sore, and bindeth up: he woundeth, and his hands make whole.

Verse 7-8

Chastisement or the lack thereof expresses two truths. 1) it is evidence that a person is a son, not a sinner {7} 2) it is evidence that a person is a sinner and not a son {8}

Verse 9

Blessed is the child who has chastening parents. Prov 13:24 He that spareth his rod hateth his son: but he that loveth him chasteneth him betimes.

Verse 10

Romans 8:28 passage

Verse 11

The fruit of chastening. The word chasten and its derivatives appears 9x (# of fruit).

1 Pet 4:1-2 Forasmuch then as Christ hath suffered for us in the flesh, arm yourselves likewise with the same mind: for he that hath suffered in the flesh hath ceased from sin; That he no longer should live the rest of *his* time in the flesh to the lusts of men, but to the will of God.

1 Pet 4:12-13 Beloved, think it not strange concerning the fiery trial which is to try you, as though some strange thing happened unto you: But rejoice, inasmuch as ye are partakers of Christ's sufferings; that, when his glory shall be revealed, ye may be glad also with exceeding joy.

Verse 12

Lift up – praise him; Praise is simply rent payment on blessings we already live in. Some of God's people are behind on their payments. Past due, in arrears, delinquent. To find the value of something you call for an appraiser.

Lift up the hands – this is what they do when they cross the finish line

Feeble knees – that is where you bend at to humble yourself. (ill) See someone running a race and they raise the hands as they cross the finish line but then they walk over to the sideline and fall down on their knees.

Verse 13

There are others watching your race and your chastening. (ill) Job's three friends – sat and watched him; judged him; criticized him; condemned him…it's easy to point the finger until you go through some things. Job 42

Phil 2:12-16

Phil 1:12-14 – Paul was in prison

Verse 14

No matter how others may treat you, you will stand before the Lord and give account of your life unto the Lord.

Verse 15

Bitterness – is a condition of the heart that will defile your life and everyone around you. If you hang around a bitter person it will either make you bitter or make you fall on your knees and beg God to help you from being bitter.

Acts 20:24 But none of these things move me, neither count I my life dear unto myself, so that I might finish my course with joy, and the ministry, which I have received of the Lord Jesus, to testify the gospel of the grace of God.

Eph 4:29-32 – bitterness in a child of God grieves the Spirit of God.

Col 3:19 Husbands, love *your* wives, and be not bitter against them.

James 3:13-16

Verse 16

Profane - "polluted, not pure; irreverent; to treat sacred things with abuse and irreverence" To be profane is to not consider the things of God with respect.

Why did he sell his birthright?

Verse 17

No place of repentance – (1828) "Sorrow for any thing done or said; the pain or grief which a person experiences in consequence of the injury or inconvenience produced by his own conduct."

The 1st mention of repentance in bible – Gen 6:6-7 - "to be sorry; to sigh; to be sorry for what you have done"

2nd use – Ex 13:17

Repentance is to change your mind – Ex 32:12, 14

God repenting and the repenting of man are in essence the same action but for different reasons. Num 23:19 God *is* not a man, that he should lie; neither the son of man, that he should repent: hath he said, and shall he not do *it*? or hath he spoken, and shall he not make it good?

God calls for man to repent – 2 Pet 3:9; Luke 13:3 I tell you, Nay: but, except ye repent, ye shall all likewise perish.

Why does man need to repent? – (He is sinfully sick) Mark 2:15-17

Will man repent on his own? – No; Rom 3:10-18

God grants repentance – 2 Tim 2:24-26

1) He calls all men to repent – Acts 17:30-31

2) He calls his people to repent - Eze 18:30 Therefore I will judge you, O house of Israel, every one according to his ways, saith the Lord GOD. Repent, and turn *yourselves* from all your transgressions; so iniquity shall not be your ruin.

3) He calls nations to repent – Jer 18:8-10 (ill) Jonah & Ninevah - Jonah 3:9-10 Who can tell *if* God will turn and repent, and turn away from his fierce anger, that we perish not? And God saw their works, that they turned from their evil way; and God repented of the evil, that he had said that he would do unto them; and he did *it* not.

4) He calls for churches to repent

Rev 2:5 – church at Ephesus, repent

Rev 2:16 – church at Pergamos, repent

Rev 3:3 – church at Sardis, repent

God treats this matter of repentance seriously.
1) Two kinds of repentance – 2 Cor 7:9-10
He will allow someone the opportunity to repent.
2 Tim 2:24-26
Rev 2:20-23
Individuals, saints of God, nations – God will grant a space of repentance. When God does this, the ball is in the individual's court – sorry they sinned or sorry they got caught and try to cover it over.
(ill) I knew a saved man who ran from God all his life. He wound up in deep sin by selling out his birthright as a child of God. He came to our church looking for a place of repentance and found none. Last time I talked to him he said, "Don't ever call me again, God is through with me, and I'm through with Him."

Verse 18-21

Mount – Exodus 19:9-25 This mount represented the giving of the law. It also represented boundaries and death if touched. Exodus 20:18-21 It also represented only fear and fright. It also was a place that the people of God did not want God to speak to them, only Moses. It was a place of burning and blackness and the worst of it all – DISTANCE from God. They could not approach unto God.

Verse 22

Sion – Difference between Zion and Sion. The word "Zion" appears 153x in OT only. Sion; 9x in both OT and NT.
Zion is a reference to the earthly place called the city of David – 2 Samuel 5:7; the city of David is Bethlehem – Luke 2:4, 11. David took from the Jebusites the fortress of Mount Zion. He "dwelt in the fort, and called it the city of David" (1 Chr. 11:7). This was the name afterwards given to the castle and royal palace on Mount Zion, as distinguished from Jerusalem

generally (1 Kings 3:1; 8:1), It was on the southwest side of Jerusalem, opposite the temple mount,

City – of the living God. The earthly Zion was CAPTURED, the heavenly Sion was CREATED.

Heavenly Jerusalem – Galatians 4:21-26 Law/Liberty; Bondage/Breaking Free; Fierceness/Freedom Revelation 21:1-2, 10-22:1-6

Angels – they were present at the giving of the law, but now they are present to minister to the saints – Hebrews 13:2

Verse 23

Church of the firstborn – Jesus is the firstborn:
Mary - Matt 1:25 And knew her not till she had brought forth her firstborn son: and he called his name JESUS.
Among brethren – Rom 8:29; Heb 1:5-6; Matt 25:40 (Acts 9:1-2, 4); John 20:17
From the dead – Col 1:18

Written in heaven – "My name is in the book of life" Phil 4:3; Rev 13:8; Rev 20:12, 15; Rev 21:27

Judge of all – Jesus; John 5:22-23 – Many judgments mentioned in Bible

Judgment seat of Christ; Judgment of the nations; Judgment of the dead

Some believe in a general judgment - Dan 12:2 And many of them that sleep in the dust of the earth shall awake, some to everlasting life, and some to shame *and* everlasting contempt.

Martha – John 11:24 Martha saith unto him, I know that he shall rise again in the resurrection of the last day.

Just men – Justified is a tremendous Bible doctrine – the Lord talking to a lawyer, "What shall I do to inherit eternal life?" Exchange about the law – this do and live. But he, willing to justify himself said, "Who is my neighbor?"

We can do one of two things in life – Justify ourselves or let God do it.

Luke 16:15 And he said unto them, Ye are they which justify yourselves before men; but God knoweth your hearts: for that which is highly esteemed among men is abomination in the sight of God.

You are not justified by what you do - Rom 3:20 Therefore by the deeds of the law there shall no flesh be justified in his sight: for by the law *is* the knowledge of sin.

Rom 3:24 Being justified freely by his grace through the redemption that is in Christ Jesus: Rom 3:26 To declare, *I say*, at this time his righteousness: that he might be just, and the justifier of him which believeth in Jesus.

"Just as though you had never sinned"

Made perfect – Jude 24-25; Rom 8:29-30

Verse 24

And to Jesus – (Verse 22, but ye are come to)

Mediator - Gal 3:20 Now a mediator is not *a mediator* of one, but God is one. 1 Tim 2:5 For *there is* one God, and one mediator between God and men, the man Christ Jesus; Job 9:32-33

New Covenant - Heb 8:6 But now hath he obtained a more excellent ministry, by how much also he is the mediator of a better covenant, which was established upon better promises. Heb 9:15 And for this cause he is the mediator of the new testament, that by means of death, for the redemption of the transgressions *that were* under the first testament, they which are called might receive the promise of eternal inheritance.

The Old Covenant was temporal; the New Covenant is eternal; and it's all because of one thing:

The Blood - Acts 20:28 Take heed therefore unto yourselves, and to all the flock, over the which the Holy Ghost hath made you overseers, to feed the church of God, which he hath purchased with his own blood. Rom 5:9 Much more then, being now justified by his blood, we shall be saved from wrath through him. Eph 1:7 In whom we have redemption through his blood, the forgiveness of sins, according to the riches of his grace; Eph

2:13 But now in Christ Jesus ye who sometimes were far off are made nigh by the blood of Christ. Col 1:20 And, having made peace through the blood of his cross, by him to reconcile all things unto himself; by him, *I say*, whether *they be* things in earth, or things in heaven. Heb 9:12 Neither by the blood of goats and calves, but by his own blood he entered in once into the holy place, having obtained eternal redemption *for us*. Heb 9:14 How much more shall the blood of Christ, who through the eternal Spirit offered himself without spot to God, purge your conscience from dead works to serve the living God? 1 Pet 1:2 Elect according to the foreknowledge of God the Father, through sanctification of the Spirit, unto obedience and sprinkling of the blood of Jesus Christ: Grace unto you, and peace, be multiplied. 1 Pet 1:18-19 Forasmuch as ye know that ye were not redeemed with corruptible things, *as* silver and gold, from your vain conversation *received* by tradition from your fathers; But with the precious blood of Christ, as of a lamb without blemish and without spot: 1 John 1:7 But if we walk in the light, as he is in the light, we have fellowship one with another, and the blood of Jesus Christ his Son cleanseth us from all sin. Rev 1:5 And from Jesus Christ, *who is* the faithful witness, *and* the first begotten of the dead, and the prince of the kings of the earth. Unto him that loved us, and washed us from our sins in his own blood, Rev 5:9-10 And they sung a new song, saying, Thou art worthy to take the book, and to open the seals thereof: for thou wast slain, and hast redeemed us to God by thy blood out of every kindred, and tongue, and people, and nation; And hast made us unto our God kings and priests: and we shall reign on the earth. Rev 12:11 And they overcame him by the blood of the Lamb, and by the word of their testimony; and they loved not their lives unto the death.

Abel's blood spoke from the ground – Vengeance; Fury; Death
Jesus' blood speaks from heaven – Victory; Forgiveness; Life

Verse 25

Escape – Directed to the saved. Hebrews 2:1-3

Phil 2:12-13 The warning? Be sure you develop an ear to hear the voice of God speaking. (ill) Our ears develop to listen to certain things – a child's voice may cry, but if we hear our child's voice utter, that voice catches our attention. Be in a room full of people talking and let a familiar voice catch your ear and immediately your attention is directed to that voice. And we need to develop an ear for the voice of God speaking to us personally and pointedly.

Verse 26

Shook earth, heaven – there will be an end to everything. An end of earth, heaven, life as we now know it…this life, as we know it, is the only time we will be able to serve the Lord by faith. In no other life will we be afforded the opportunity to live by faith.

(ill) Thomas - John 20:29 Jesus saith unto him, Thomas, because thou hast seen me, thou hast believed: blessed *are* they that have not seen, and *yet* have believed. We say show us and we will believe, Jesus says believe and I'll show you. That is the PRINCIPLE of living by faith.

Verse 27

Shaken – Ps 18:7-10; Joel 2:10-11 When? Matt 24:29-30; Rev 6:13

Cannot be shaken – the Kingdom of God (verse 28) everything else will be gone and all that will remain will be the KOG and its contents.

(ill) The disciples wanted to show Jesus all the buildings of the temple, Matt 24:2 And Jesus said unto them, See ye not all these things? verily I say unto you, There shall not be left here one stone upon another, that shall not be thrown down.

Verse 28

The KOG - Matt 6:33 But seek ye first the kingdom of God, and his righteousness; and all these things shall be added unto you. Luke 17:21 Neither shall they say, Lo here! or, lo there! for, behold, the kingdom of God is within you. John 3:3 Jesus answered and said unto him, Verily, verily, I say unto thee, Except a man be born again, he cannot see the kingdom of God. John 3:5 Jesus answered, Verily, verily, I say unto thee, Except a man be born of water and *of* the Spirit, he cannot enter into the kingdom of God. Rom 14:17 For the kingdom of God is not meat and drink; but righteousness, and peace, and joy in the Holy Ghost.

You can blow away my home, my church, but you cannot shake the Lord inside of me. (ill) "Lock me up in a prison, throw away the key - but as long as I have Jesus then I can still go free!"

Serve acceptably – Rom 12:1-2; Rom 14:12-18; Eph 5:8-12

Verse 29

Consuming Fire – the end of all things without Christ – 2 Pet 3:10-15 The salvation of souls and the growth of a child of God are the most important thing in this life. How much we have in the bank account, what company we worked with, how much retirement we have in our 401k, how many friends like us on FB, how many follow us on twitter - all of that is irrelevant in light of eternity. This world lieth in darkness and a little light will dispel all darkness but when it is all over – Rev 20:15 and there will be those there that we could had made a difference – Jude 22-23

CHAPTER 13

Verse 1

John Phillips – "The Christian life is a practical life, and the driving force behind everything is love. Love first conceived salvation's plan in a past eternity. Love brought the Son of God from heaven to die for sinners on a cross. Love is shed abroad in the hearts of believers by the Spirit of God. Love led the writer of this letter to take his pen and pour out his heart, urging, pleading with those professing the Christian faith to prove their profession to be real by going on."

Brotherly love continue – "let it endure, let it remain, let it stand, let it permeate, let it be steadfast"

1 John 3:14-18

"You can give without loving, but it is impossible for you to love and not give."

1 Thes 4:9 But as touching brotherly love ye need not that I write unto you: for ye yourselves are taught of God to love one another.

1 John 4:7-21

> To dwell above, with saints in love
> That will indeed be glory;
> To dwell below, with saints we know –
> Well, that's another story!

Inside of us who are saved, dwells the Holy Spirit to teach us to love with the perfected love of God working in us; and in context 1 John 4:4…because greater is he that is in you, than he that is in the world.

Rom 12:14-21

1 Pet 3:8-9

1 Pet 2:17 Honour all *men*. Love the brotherhood. Fear God. Honour the king.

Jas 2:8 If ye fulfil the royal law according to the scripture, Thou shalt love thy neighbour as thyself, ye do well:

Verse 2
Angels – interesting insertion about angels in the context of brotherly love continuing.
Strangers – people you do not know; someone strange to you.
Entertained – "to be a host to" (ill) Judges 13

Verse 3
Remember – Verse 1 Remember the Saints; Verse 2 Remember the Strangers; Verse 3 Remember the Sufferers – 1 Cor 12:12-14, 26
Rom 12:15 Rejoice with them that do rejoice, and weep with them that weep.
When you do, don't expect this in return – Ps 35:11-17 – learn to call upon the name of the Lord! Context of Ps 35 gives us a glimpse of the life of Jesus Christ.

Verse 4
Marriage – a redefined institution in the world – a set standard in the Bible. Chastity is under attack today and viewed as "weird, stupid and uncool" among our society. Hollywood, TV, and the media all venerate immorality and permissiveness. Every moral restraint is attacked and portrayed as old fashioned and unfashionable in the eyes of the world. But we will not be judged by the world –
Isa 5:20-21 Woe unto them that call evil good, and good evil; that put darkness for light, and light for darkness; that put bitter for sweet, and sweet for bitter! Woe unto *them that are* wise in their own eyes, and prudent in their own sight!

Verse 5

Conversation – don't talk to try and get something. Poor mouthing, hoping that someone will hear and give you a hand out.

I will never leave THEE – God wants every child of God to experience Him supplying your needs. Php 4:19 But my God shall supply all your need according to his riches in glory by Christ Jesus. Matthew 6:25-33

Verse 6

Boldly say – your testimony about what God has done in your life. "The Lord is my helper" – almost sounds like Psalm 23.
(ill) Many years ago in a small town in Virginia, the newspaper printed the upcoming sermon topics for the local churches. A pastor phoned the editor to share that his sermon for the upcoming Sunday would be titled, "The Lord is my Shepherd". The editor asked, "Is that all?" To which the pastor replied, "That's enough." When the paper arrived at his home he opened it to find the printed topic: "The Lord is My Shepherd and That's Enough."

Verse 7-9

Remember – Eph 4:11-14; 2 Tim 4:1-4 I charge *thee* therefore before God, and the Lord Jesus Christ, who shall judge the quick and the dead at his appearing and his kingdom; Preach the word; be instant in season, out of season; reprove, rebuke, exhort with all longsuffering and doctrine. For the time will come when they will not endure sound doctrine; but after their own lusts shall they heap to themselves teachers, having itching ears; And they shall turn away *their* ears from the truth, and shall be turned unto fables.
1 Pet 5
3 times in closing chapter of Hebrews 13 – 7, 17, 24

"Those who handle the word of God with skill and in the power of the Holy Spirit are engaged in the highest and most noble profession on earth."

1 Tim 5:17-18 Let the elders that rule well be counted worthy of double honour, especially they who labour in the word and doctrine. For the scripture saith, Thou shalt not muzzle the ox that treadeth out the corn. And, The labourer *is* worthy of his reward.

Faith Follow – 1 Cor 4:15-16 For though ye have ten thousand instructors in Christ, yet *have ye* not many fathers: for in Christ Jesus I have begotten you through the gospel. Wherefore I beseech you, be ye followers of me.

1 Cor 11:1-2 Be ye followers of me, even as I also *am* of Christ. Now I praise you, brethren, that ye remember me in all things, and keep the ordinances, as I delivered *them* to you.

Jesus, The Same – Yesterday Jesus helped me; Today He did the same. How long will this continue? Forever, praise His name!

Meats – Deep, Debatable, Dead doctrines. The thing that is really dividing the body of Christ today – the rapture, does it happen before, during, after the tribulation. Will the church go through the tribulation? We are told to rightly divide the Word of God.

(ill) The body of Christ is literally, really a part of Jesus Christ. The tribulation is known as a time of the wrath of God. Matt 25, as much as you have done it unto one of the least of these my brethren, you have done it unto me. Acts 9, Saul on Damascus Road, Why persecutest thou me? If the church goes through the tribulation, that means that God will pouring out His wrath upon his Son.

Verse 10

Altar – he is referring to the OT altar and the restrictions that accompanied that altar.

Verse 11

Bodies for sin – The OT offerings were of two kinds, 1) Sweet-savor offerings, which became food for the priests. 2) Sin offerings, which were burned and never eaten or enjoyed.

Verse 12

Suffered – 1 Peter 4:1-2, 12-19

Verse 13

Let us – One of the themes of Hebrews – Let us fear, let us labor, let us come boldly, let us hold fast, let us go on, let us draw near, let us consider one another, let us lay aside every weight, let us run the race, let us offer…
Let us go where he went – the place of sacrifice;
Reproach – "shame; disgrace; contempt"

Verse 14

Continuing City – this world will pass away one day; 2 Pet 3:10-11. Here I do have a city, but not a continuing city. This world is not our world –

Verse 15

Sacrifice of praise – 1 Thes 5:18 In every thing give thanks: for this is the will of God in Christ Jesus concerning you. Eph 5:20 Giving thanks always for all things unto God and the Father in the name of our Lord Jesus Christ;

Verse 16

Do good - Tit 3:8 *This is* a faithful saying, and these things I will that thou affirm constantly, that they which have believed in God might be careful to maintain good works. These things are good and profitable unto men.
Lip service is not enough; "Do" service is better

1John 3:18 My little children, let us not love in word, neither in tongue; but in deed and in truth.

Verse 17
Ref verse 7, 24

Verse 18
Pray for us – 1 Sam 12:23 Moreover as for me, God forbid that I should sin against the LORD in ceasing to pray for you: but I will teach you the good and the right way:

Good conscience – 1 Tim 1:5 Now the end of the commandment is charity out of a pure heart, and *of* a good conscience, and *of* faith unfeigned:

Before God - Acts 23:1 And Paul, earnestly beholding the council, said, Men *and* brethren, I have lived in all good conscience before God until this day.

Exercise - "to practice; to work at" Acts 24:16 And herein do I exercise myself, to have always a conscience void of offence toward God, and *toward* men.

Living before others - 2 Cor 4:2 But have renounced the hidden things of dishonesty, not walking in craftiness, nor handling the word of God deceitfully; but by manifestation of the truth commending ourselves to every man's conscience in the sight of God.

1 Tim 4:1-2 Now the Spirit speaketh expressly, that in the latter times some shall depart from the faith, giving heed to seducing spirits, and doctrines of devils; Speaking lies in hypocrisy; having their conscience seared with a hot iron;

Verse 20-21
Good works - Tit 2:14 Who gave himself for us, that he might redeem us from all iniquity, and purify unto himself a peculiar people, zealous of good works. Matt 5:16 Let your light so shine

before men, that they may see your good works, and glorify your Father which is in heaven.

Verse 22
In few words – 6,913 words to be exact!

Verse 25
Grace be with you all. Amen
A great way to end a letter, a better way to end a life – Grace!

www.ingramcontent.com/pod-product-compliance
Lightning Source LLC
LaVergne TN
LVHW051243080426
835513LV00016B/1717